OCEANIA
Geography Activity Book

Maps, Facts, Flags, Activities:
Learn About the Countries of Oceania

Published by Dylanna Press an imprint of Dylanna Publishing, Inc.
Copyright © 2024 by Dylanna Press

All rights reserved. No part of this publication may be reproduced, stored in a retrieval system, or transmitted by any means, including electronic, mechanical, photocopying, or otherwise, without prior written permission of the publisher.

Limit of liability/Disclaimer of Warranty: The Publisher and the author make no representations or warranties with respect to the accuracy or completeness of the contents of this work and specifically disclaim all warranties, including without limitation warranties of fitness for a particular purpose.

Although the publisher has taken all reasonable care in the preparation of this book, we make no warranty about the accuracy or completeness of its content and, to the maximum extent permitted, disclaim all liability arising from its use.

Trademarks: Dylanna Press is a registered trademark of Dylanna Publishing, Inc. and may not be used without written permission.

Image credits: Cook Islands coat of arms: Josedar, CC BY-SA 4.0 <https://creativecommons.org/licenses/by-sa/4.0>, via Wikimedia Commons; Fiji coat of arms: Simi Tukidia, CC BY-SA 3.0 https://creativecommons.org/licenses/by-sa/3.0>, via Wikimedia Commons; New Caledonia national emblem: J.delanoy, CC BY 1.0 <https://creativecommons.org/licenses/by/1.0>, via Wikimedia Commons; New Zealand coat of arms: Sodacan, CC BY-SA 3.0 https://creativecommons.org/licenses/by-sa/3.0>, via Wikimedia Commons; Niue coat of arms: Euroman3, Public domain, via Wikimedia Commons; Norfolk Island coat of arms: Squiresy92 including elements from Sodacan, CC BY-SA 4.0 <https://creativecommons.org/licenses/by-sa/4.0>, via Wikimedia Commons; Northern Mariana Islands quarter: United States Mint, Public domain, via Wikimedia Commons; Samoa coat of arms: Simitukidia, CC BY-SA 3.0 <https://creativecommons.org/licenses/by-sa/3.0>, via Wikimedia Commons; Solomon Islands coat of arms:- By Prez001 - Own work, CC BY-SA 3.0, https://commons.wikimedia.org/w/index.php?curid=29301427; Tuvalu coat of arms:- By Denelson83 - Own work, CC BY-SA 3.0, https://commons.wikimedia.org/w/index.php?curid=5442520; Vanuatu coat of arms: By Sodacan - Own work, CC BY-SA 3.0, https://commons.wikimedia.org/w/index.php?curid=20046125; Wallis and Futuna coat of arms: This image includes elements that have been taken or adapted from this file: File:Great_Seal_of_France.svg, CC BY-SA 3.0, https://commons.wikimedia.org/w/index.php?curid=122855329

Editor: Julie Grady

Welcome to Oceania

The region of Oceania is made up of thousands of islands spread across the Pacific Ocean. It includes Australia, which is the smallest continent by land mass and the microcontinent of Zealandia, home to New Zealand. Oceania encompasses a land area of approximately 3.3 million square miles (8.5 million square kilometers). It is made up of 14 recognized countries as well 11 additional territories and dependencies. The total population is approximately 46 million (as of 2024).

Oceania is divided into four regions:

Australasia, which includes Australia, New Zealand, and Norfolk Island.

Melanesia, which includes Fiji, New Caledonia, Papua New Guinea, Solomon Islands, and Vanuatu.

Micronesia, which includes Guam, Kiribat, Marshall Islands, Federated States of Micronesia, Nauru, Northern Mariana Islands, and Palau.

Polynesia, which includes American Samoa, Cook Islands, French Polynesia, Niue, Pitcairn Islands, Samoa, Tokelau, Tonga, Tuvalu, and Wallis and Futuna.

While there are numerous languages spoken across Oceania, some of the most widely spoken include English, French, Fijian, Samoan, Gilbertese, Tongan, Tahitian, and Maori. Christianity is the dominant religion, including Protestantism and Catholicism. Other religions include Islam, Hinduism, and indigenous religions.

Oceania is also home to many unique flora and fauna, some found nowhere else in the world. Birds are especially diverse, with species such as kiwis, emus, and various seabirds. Native mammals include iconic marsupials like kangaroos and koalas, and unique animals such as the platypus and echidna.

The marine life around Oceania is just as impressive, with the Great Barrier Reef off the coast of Australia being the world's largest coral reef system. This reef, along with others in the region, supports a vast array of marine species.

As you explore Oceania through this activity book, you'll learn about its diverse geography, vibrant cultures, an d incredible wildlife. Get ready to embark on an adventure across the islands of the Pacific!

Oceania countries and territories included in this book:

1. American Samoa (US territory)
2. Australia
3. Cook Islands (Associated state of New Zealand)
4. Federated States of Micronesia
5. Fiji
6. French Polynesia (French overseas collectivity)
7. Guam (US territory)
8. Kiribati
9. Marshall Islands
10. Nauru
11. New Caledonia (French territory)
12. New Zealand
13. Niue (Associated state of New Zealand)
14. Norfolk Island (Australian external territory)
15. Northern Mariana Islands (US territory)
16. Palau
17. Papua New Guinea
18. Pitcairn Islands (British Overseas Territory)
19. Samoa
20. Solomon Islands
21. Tokelau (Territory of New Zealand)
22. Tonga
23. Tuvalu
24. Vanuatu
25. Wallis and Futuna (French overseas collectivity)

Map Activity
Use the map to answer the questions below.

1. Which country in Oceania is the largest by land area? _____
2. Which countries are neighbors to Nauru? _____
3. Which country is farthest to the south in Oceania? _____
4. Is New Zealand larger than Papua New Guinea? _____
5. Which ocean is to the south of Australia? _____
6. Which islands are located farthest east? _____
7. Which sea lies to the west of New Zealand? _____
8. Can you name three island nations in the South Pacific Ocean? _____

AMERICAN SAMOA

American Samoa, a territory of the United States since 1900, is located in the South Pacific Ocean. It consists of five islands and two atolls, with a rich history that dates back over 3,000 years, when the Samoan culture first developed. The capital, Pago Pago, is known for its natural deep harbor. American Samoa's culture blends traditional Samoan ways with American influences, offering a unique experience of festivities, nature, and history to explore.

Tutuila

PAGO PAGO

Ofu   Olosega
Ta'u
Manu'a Islands

AMERICAN SAMOA
(UNITED STATES)

Facts About American Samoa

Capital:	Pago Pago
National Motto:	Samoa — let God be first
Area:	76.83 square miles (199 square kilometers)
Islands:	Tutuila, Aunu`u, Ofu, Olosega, Ta`u, Rose Atoll, and Swains Island
Population:	45,035
Bordering Countries:	Maritime borders with Samoa, Tonga, Cook Islands, Niue, and Tokelau
Languages:	Samoan, English
Major Landmarks:	Cape Taputapu, Fogama'a Crater, Matafao Peak, Rainmaker Mountain
Famous Samoans:	Tulsi Gabbard (politician), Mighty Mo (boxer), Musashimaru Kōyō (wrestler)

Country Flag

Did You Know?

- Tutuila Island is known for its high consumption of fast food.
- In 1966, the UN offered independence, but the vote favored remaining a U.S. territory.
- Known as "Football Island," it has an exceptionally high rate of NFL players per capita.
- Tuna canning is a major industry, employing about 80% of the workforce.
- It consists of five volcanic islands and two coral atolls.
- Hosts the greatest marine biodiversity in the U.S. with over 250 coral species and 930 fish species.
- Features endemic plant species and 35 native bird species.
- Home to three bat species, all considered threatened or endangered.
- The Samoan flying fox, a local bat, has a 3-foot wingspan.
- Encompasses rich rainforests, significantly impacted by cyclones and logging.

Where in the world is American Samoa ...

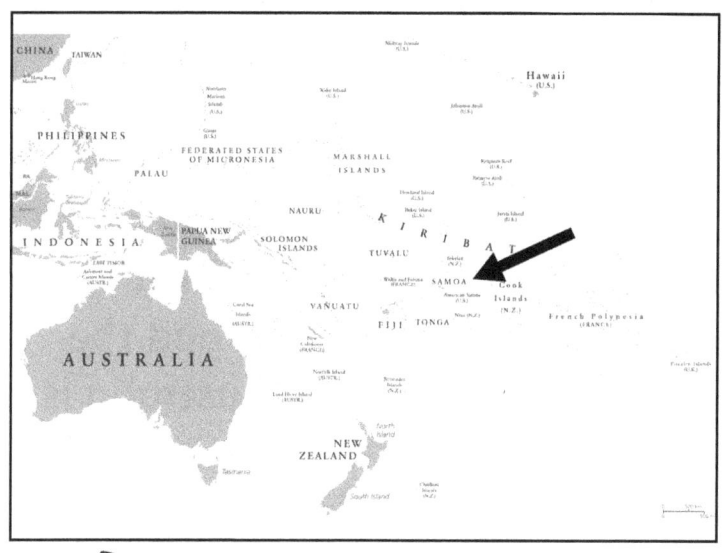

American Samoan fruit bat

Crossword Puzzle

Across

3 American Samoa's favorite fast food? It swims in cans!
5 American Samoa is famous for producing players for this sport
7 Ocean where American Samoa is located
9 The capital of American Samoa
10 A bat with a wingspan as wide as an owl's

Down

1 Island home of coral that's more colorful than a rainbow
2 Symbol on American Samoan flag
4 American Samoa is a territory of which country?
6 This island in American Samoa is known for having a lot of fast food
8 American Samoa consists of five volcanic islands and two of these

AUSTRALIA

Australia is known as the "Land Down Under" because it's located in the southern hemisphere of our planet. It's famous for its unique animals like kangaroos and koalas, beautiful beaches, and the Great Barrier Reef, the largest coral reef in the world. Australia is also home to the Outback, a vast, remote area with stunning landscapes. People from all over the world visit Australia to see its natural wonders and vibrant cities like Sydney and Melbourne.

Facts About Australia

Capital:	Canberra
National Motto:	No official motto
Area:	2.969 million square miles (7.692 million square kilometers)
Major Cities:	Sydney, Melbourne, Brisbane, Perth, Adelaide
Population:	25.69 million
Bordering Countries:	Maritime borders with East Timor, Indonesia, New Zealand, Papua New Guinea, Solomon Islands, and New Caledonia
Language:	English
Major Landmarks:	Sydney Opera House, Great Barrier Reef, Uluru (Ayers Rock), The Twelve Apostles
Famous Australians:	Hugh Jackman (actor), Steve Irwin (conservationist), Cate Blanchett (actress)

Country Flag

Did You Know?

- Australia is HUGE: It's the world's sixth-largest country, so big you could fit all of Europe (excluding Russian portion) inside it!
- Lots of Beaches: With over 10,000 beaches, you could visit a new beach every day for over 27 years!
- The Daintree Rainforest is over 180 million years old – dinosaurs roamed here!
- Australia has animals you won't find anywhere else, like kangaroos, koalas, and platypuses.
- The Great Barrier Reef: It's the largest coral reef system in the world – so big you can see it from space!
- Weirdly Pink Lake: Lake Hillier looks like a bubble gum milkshake because it's bright pink, but scientists still aren't sure why.
- Lots of Camels: Australia has the world's largest population of wild camels with one hump.
- Big Rock in the Desert: Uluru (Ayers Rock) is a massive sandstone rock in the heart of the Australian Outback that's sacred to indigenous Australians.
- The oldest evidence of life on Earth, fossilized bacteria, was found in Western Australia, dating back about 3.5 billion years.
- The "Dingo Fence" is one of the longest structures in the world, stretching 5,614 km (about 3,488 miles) to keep dingoes away from fertile land.
- The Sydney Opera House roof is made of over 1 million tiles that look like sails from ships that once came to Sydney Harbour.

Where in the world is Australia ...

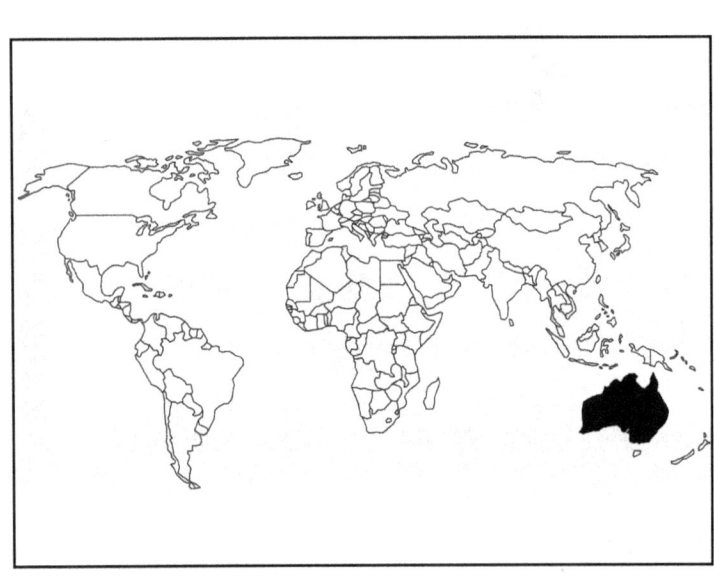

Kangaroo

Australia is home to many unique animals. Read each description and look for clues about the animal's appearance, behavior, or special features. Draw a line from each animal picture to the matching description.

1. This hopping marsupial uses its powerful hind legs to travel great distances and carries its baby in a pouch.
2. This fluffy, tree-dwelling animal sleeps for up to 20 hours a day and only eats eucalyptus leaves.
3. This unique mammal has a duck-like bill, webbed feet, and lays eggs.
4. This wild dog is known for its golden fur and haunting howl, often found roaming the Australian outback.
5. This giant bird can't fly but can run incredibly fast on its long legs, making it a speedy sprinter.
6. This burrowing marsupial has a chunky body and strong claws, perfect for digging tunnels underground.
7. This small, fierce marsupial is known for its loud screeches and powerful bite, living only on the island of Tasmania.
8. This spiny mammal has a long, sticky tongue for catching ants and termites and is one of the few egg-laying mammals.
9. The largest reptile in the world, this fearsome predator can grow up to 7 meters long and is found in northern Australia's rivers and coasts.
10. Known for its loud, laughing call, this bird often sits in trees watching for prey like insects and small reptiles.

COOK ISLANDS

The Cook Islands are a collection of 15 small islands in the Pacific Ocean. They're famous for their clear blue waters, white sandy beaches, and colorful coral reefs. The islands are home to lots of interesting sea creatures and have mountains for exploring too. People from around the world come to the Cook Islands to enjoy the beautiful scenery and learn about the local culture, which includes music, dance, and art.

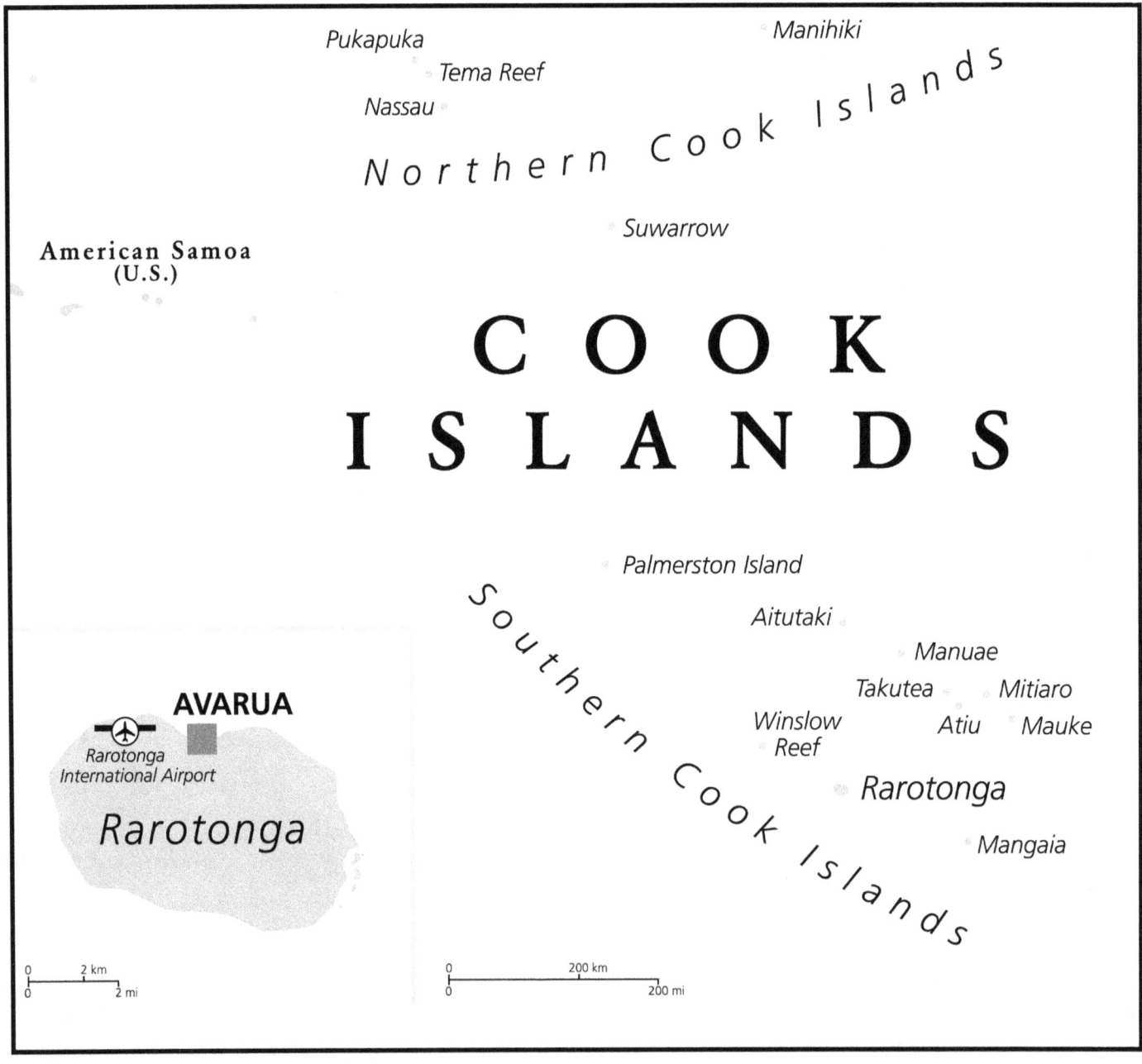

Facts About Cook Islands

Capital:	Avarua
National Motto:	No official motto
Area:	91.4 square miles (236.7 square kilometers)
Islands:	Aitutaki, Atiu, Mangaia, Manihiki, Mauke, Mitiaro, Nassau, Palmerston, Penrhyn, Pukapuka, Rakahanga, Rarotonga, Suwarrow, Takutea, Tongareva
Population:	17,065
Bordering Countries:	Maritime borders with American Samoa, French Polynesia, Samoa
Language:	English, Cook Islands Māori
Major Landmarks:	Aitutaki Lagoon, Te Rua Manga (The Needle), Muri Lagoon
Famous Cook Islanders:	Sir Thomas Davis (prime minister), Albert Henry (politician), Piltz Napa (artist), Margharet Matenga (environmentalist)

Country Flag

Did You Know?

- The Cook Islands are made up of 15 islands scattered over 2 million square kilometers of the Pacific Ocean, but the land area is just about the size of Washington D.C.!
- Stone Giants: There are ancient stone figures called "Marae" that are similar to the famous Easter Island statues but much less known.
- The islands are surrounded by one of the world's largest coral reefs, making it a paradise for snorkelers and divers.
- British explorer Captain James Cook visited the islands in the 1770s, which is how they got their name, but he wasn't the first to discover them.
- The islands are so fertile they can grow fruits like coconuts, papayas, and pineapples in abundance.
- The Cook Islands have a vast exclusive economic zone, rich in marine biodiversity and potential underwater treasures.
- From July to October, humpback whales can be seen near the islands, where they come to give birth.
- Rarotonga, the main island, has one main road that circles the entire island. You can drive around it in less than an hour!
- Cook Islanders speak Cook Islands Maori, also known as Rarotongan, which has several dialects unique to each island.
- The Cook Islands are one of the few places in the world without a McDonald's.
- They use coins that have water creatures on them, like fish, turtles, and even sharks!

Where in the world are Cook Islands ...

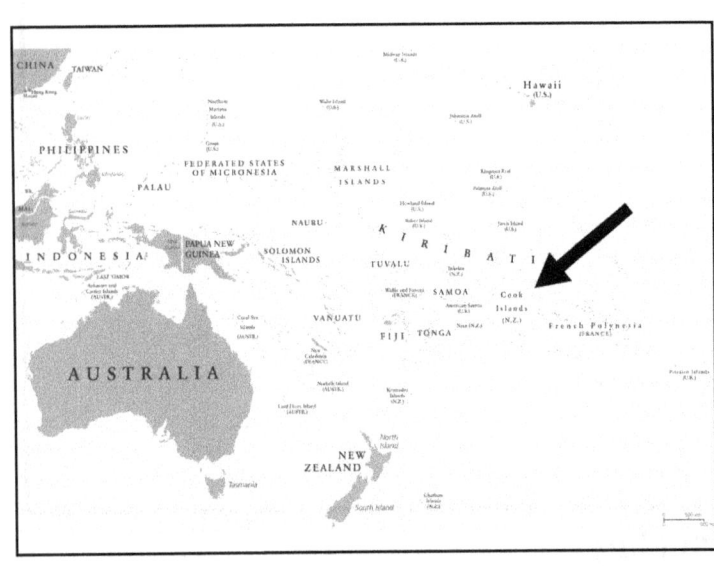

Red-tailed Tropicbird

Vaka traditional canoe

Coat of arms

Word Search

AITUTAKI LAGOON
AVARUA
BIODIVERSITY
CORAL REEFS
JAMES COOK
MAORI
MARAE
PACIFIC
RAROTONGA
TROPICBIRD
VAKA
WHALES

```
F T V V I R O A M A B B H K N
U B I O D I V E R S I T Y O K
E S T J G T G V V K W L O H E
L W F K A W H F K K Y G Q A H
R A U M P M I X I X A S O S S
A Z V F I V E I N L A J D F W
R T Z A H Q E S I R R A R E H
O H R G R A S K C V Q K R E A
T K I T R U A D O O O A J R L
O R S A P T A E O W O V G L E
N I M V U H S R U C W K P A S
G M H T V F M N P Y R J C R D
A Q I V E E M D S R G Z I O J
F A B T V C P A C I F I C C X
S C G A A D R I B C I P O R T
```

FEDERATED STATES OF MICRONESIA

The Federated States of Micronesia is a country made up of over 600 islands spread across the western Pacific Ocean. It's known for its palm-lined beaches, ancient ruins, and diverse marine life, making it a fantastic place for snorkeling and diving. The islands have a rich history and culture, with traditional customs still a big part of daily life. Visitors can explore the rainforests, climb volcanic mountains, and learn about the local way of life in the small villages scattered across the islands.

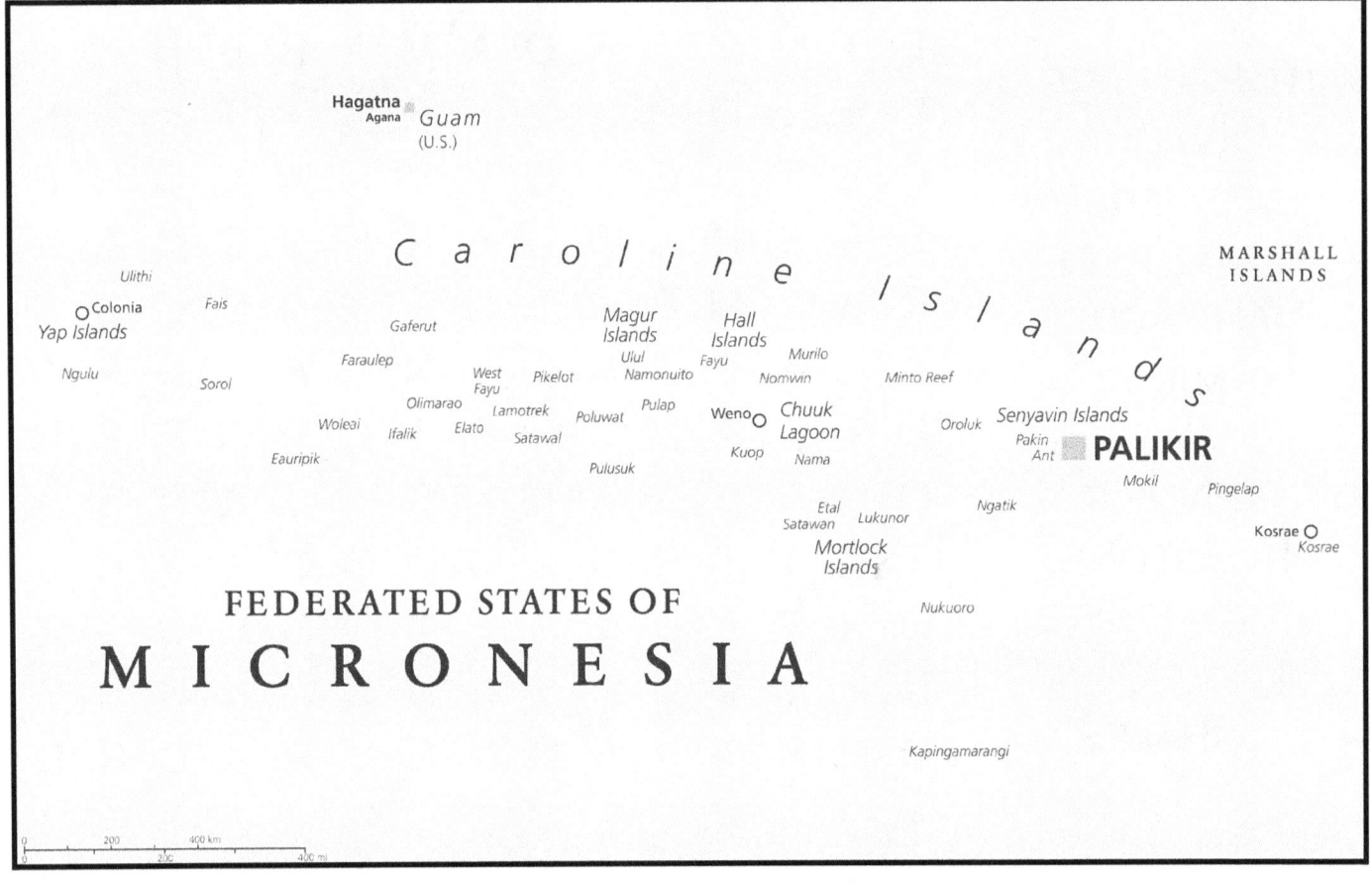

Facts About Federated States of Micronesia

Capital:	Palikir
National Motto:	Peace, Unity, Liberty
Area:	271 square miles (702 square kilometers)
Major Cities:	Weno, Palikir, Tofol, Colonia
Population:	113,131
Bordering Countries:	Maritime borders with the Marshall Islands, Palau, Papua New Guinea, and Guam (United States)
Languages:	Chuuk, Kosraean, Ponapean, Yapese, English
Major Landmarks:	Nan Madol, Truk (Chuuk) Lagoon, Sokehs Rock
Famous Micronesians:	Wesley Simina (president), John Haglelgam (politician), Nicole Yamase (scientist)

Country Flag

Did You Know?

- Nan Madol on Pohnpei is often called the "Venice of the Pacific." It's an ancient city built on a series of artificial islets, linked by canals and home to massive stone ruins.
- Yap is famous for its giant stone money called Rai, some as large as 12 feet in diameter, used for traditional transactions and as a form of wealth.
- Chuuk Lagoon is a world-renowned diving site, known for its "Ghost Fleet" of over 60 ships, planes, and submarines sunk during World War II.
- Mount Nanlaud on Pohnpei is the highest peak in Micronesia, offering lush trails and stunning views for adventurous hikers.
- Traditional tattoos are an important part of Micronesian culture, with each island having its own unique designs that signify social status, community, and identity.
- In parts of Micronesia, society is traditionally matriarchal, with women playing key roles in family and community leadership.
- A local delicacy is the breadfruit, which can be eaten in various ways, but is often roasted, boiled, or turned into a sweet dessert.

Where in the world is Micronesia ...

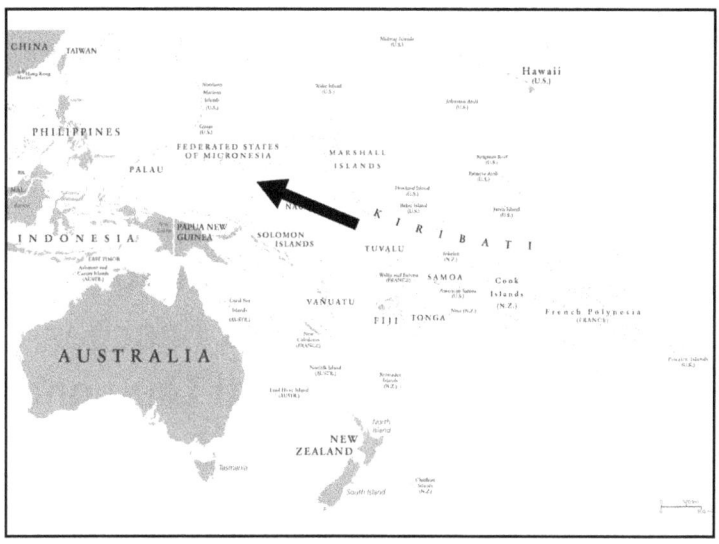

Chuuk Flying Fox

Rai Stones

Animal Matching

Micronesia is home to many interesting animals. Read the description of each animal and write the correct name under the picture.

- **Coconut Crab** - Known for its ability to climb trees and crack open coconuts, this large terrestrial crab is a common sight on the islands
- **Sea Turtle** - Common in the waters around the islands, these turtles are often seen nesting on the beaches
- **Humphead Wrasse** - A large and colorful fish commonly found in the coral reefs surrounding the islands.
- **Reef Shark** - Several species of reef sharks inhabit the waters of Micronesia, often seen by divers exploring the coral reefs.
- **Kingfisher** - A small bird with a striking blue and orange plumage, found in the forests of the islands
- **Giant Clam** - Found in the coral reefs, these clams are known for their large size and vibrant mantle colors.

FIJI

Fiji is a country in the South Pacific made up of more than 300 islands. It's famous for its rugged landscapes, palm-lined beaches, and coral reefs with clear lagoons. The main islands, Viti Levu and Vanua Levu, are where most Fijians live and you can find rainforests and waterfalls to explore. Fiji is known for its friendly people, vibrant culture, and outdoor adventures like snorkeling, surfing, and diving. Visitors love Fiji for its tropical beauty and the chance to learn about its interesting traditions and customs.

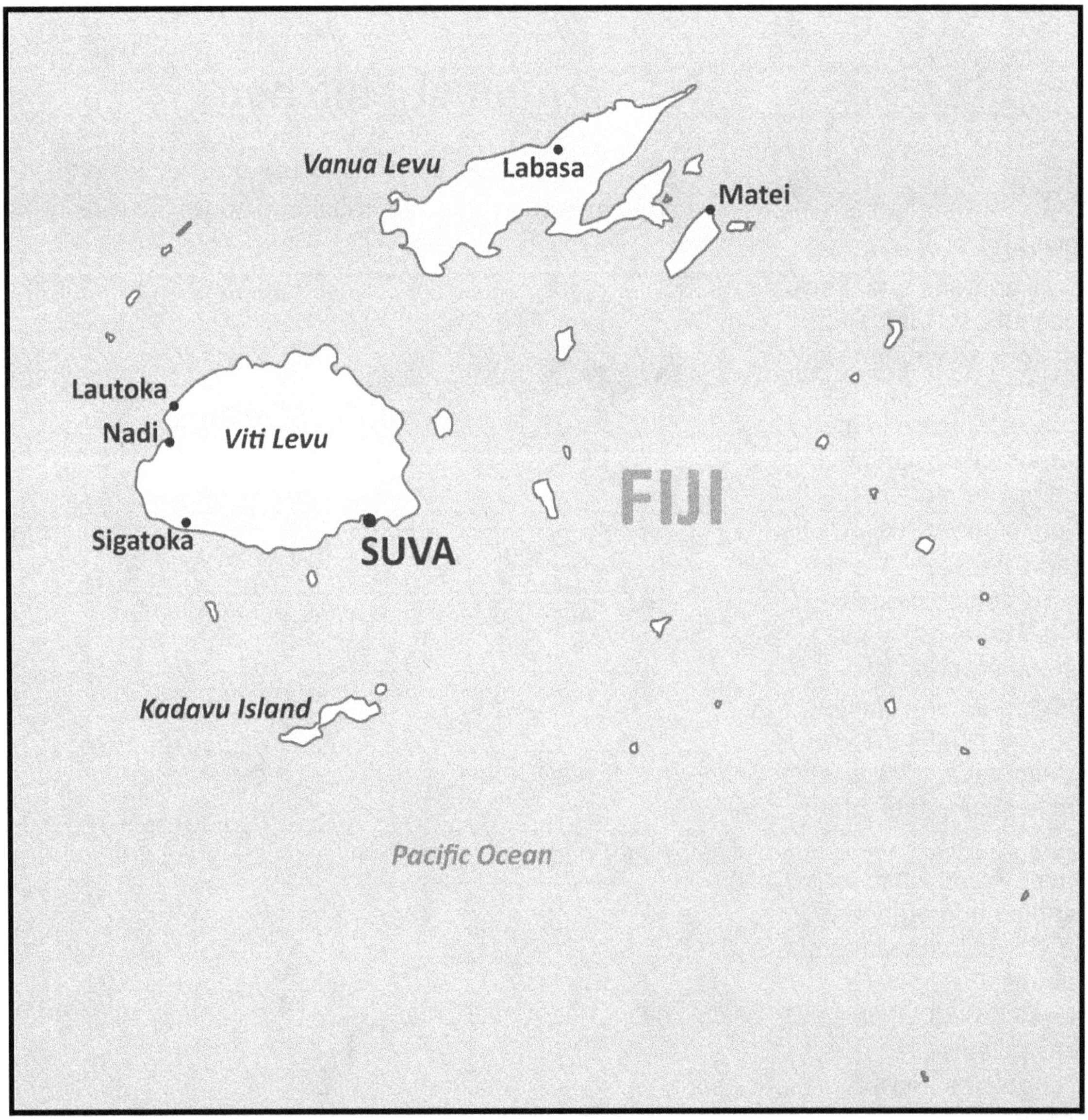

Facts About Fiji

Capital:	Suva
National Motto:	Fear God and Honor the Queen
Area:	7,054 square miles (18,270 square kilometers)
Major Cities:	Suva, Lautoka, Nadi
Population:	924,610
Bordering Countries:	Vanuatu, Tonga, and Samoa
Languages:	English, Fijian, and Fiji Hindi
Major Landmarks:	Great Astrolabe Reef, Sri Siva Subramaniya Temple, Bouma National Heritage Park, Sigatoka Sand Dunes National Park
Famous Fijians:	Waisale Serevi (rugby player), Roy Krishna (footballer), Satendra Nandan (author), Laisenia Qarase (politician)

Country Flag

Did You Know?

- Fiji is an archipelago of more than 330 islands, but less than a third are inhabited. It's surrounded by vast expanses of the Pacific Ocean.
- Known as the "Soft Coral Capital of the World," Fiji's waters are home to an astounding array of colorful corals and diverse marine life, making it a diver's paradise.
- Taveuni Island in Fiji is one of the few places where you can stand with one foot in today and the other in yesterday, thanks to the International Date Line.
- One of the world's most famous brands of bottled water comes from an artesian aquifer in Fiji.
- The Sawau tribe on Beqa Island is renowned for their traditional practice of fire walking, which has fascinated people for centuries.
- Fiji is at the forefront of sustainable tourism in the Pacific, with numerous eco-resorts and conservation initiatives protecting its natural environment.
- Kava, a traditional drink made from the ground root of the kava plant, plays a central role in Fijian culture, used in ceremonies and social gatherings.

Coat of arms

Where in the world is Fiji ...

Kava Ceremony

Bure - A traditional Fijian home made of wood, bamboo, and thatched with palm leaves

Crossword Puzzle

Across

4. Traditional Fijian communal meeting house
5. The group of islands Fiji belongs to
8. Popular drink made from a root in Fiji
9. Fiji is known for this kind of stunning natural coastline
10. One of the main islands of Fiji

Down

1. Popular fruit grown in Fiji
2. Fiji's capital city
3. Traditional Fijian ceremonial dance
6. The ocean surrounding Fiji
7. Famous Fijian rugby player, Waisale _____

FRENCH POLYNESIA

French Polynesia is a collection of 118 islands in the South Pacific Ocean, celebrated for its picturesque overwater bungalows, clear blue seas, and vibrant coral reefs. Among these islands, Tahiti and Bora Bora are especially famous for their incredible underwater life and stunning landscapes. The culture here is alive with traditional music, dance, and crafts that reflect the islands' rich heritage. Adventure awaits around every corner, whether it's snorkeling in the lagoon, hiking up lush mountain trails, or discovering ancient temples. For the people of French Polynesia, the connection to nature and the sea is a vital part of daily life.

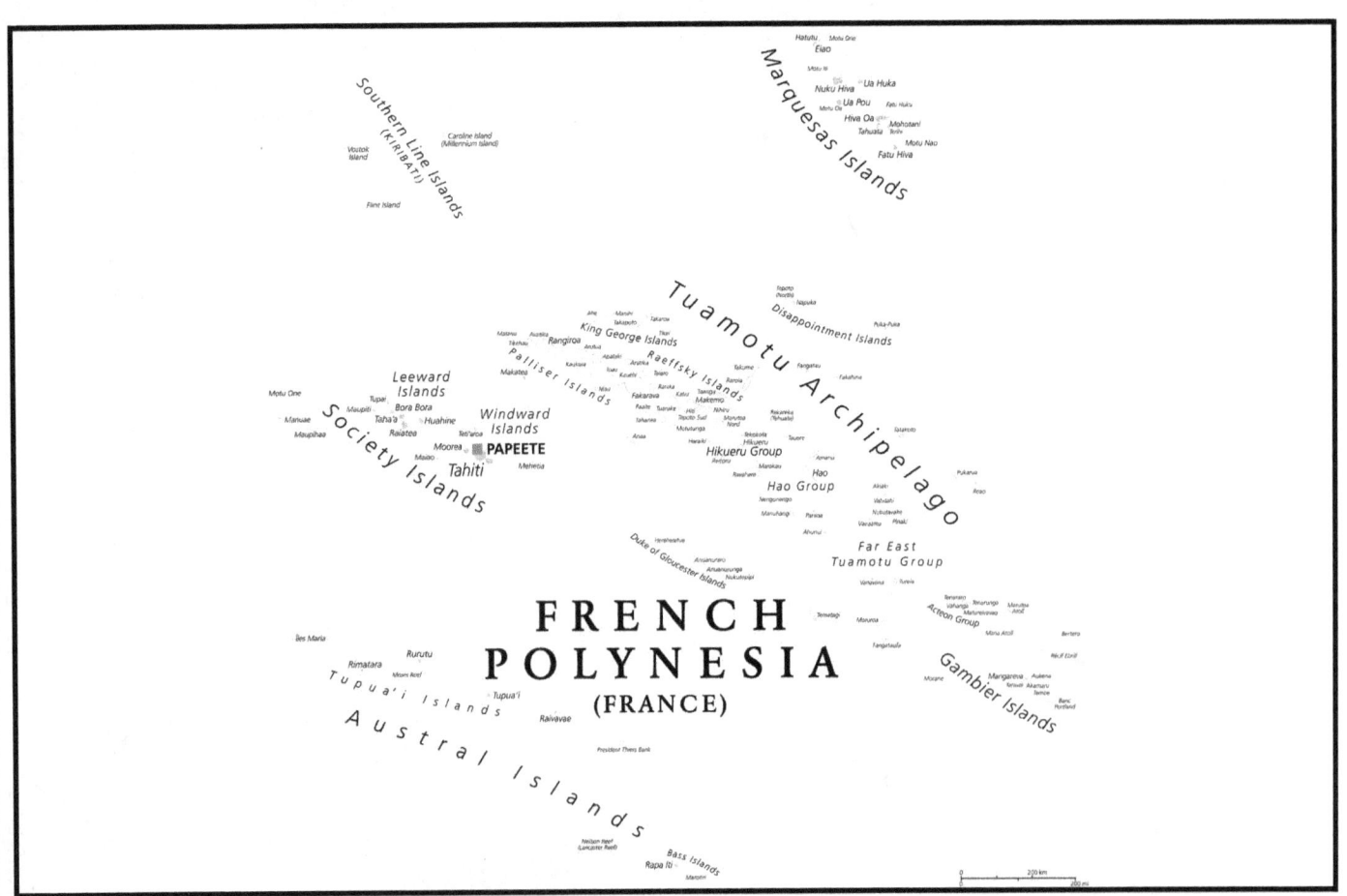

Facts About French Polynesia

Capital: Papeete
National Motto: Liberty, Equality, Fraternity
Area: 3,521 square kilometers (1,359 sq mi)

Major Islands: Bora Bora, Moorea, Huahine, Raiatea, Tahaa, Tahiti

Population: 308,872
Bordering Countries: New Zealand (sea border)
Languages: French, Tahitian
Major Landmarks: Mount Otemanu, Cook's Bay, Fakarava, Rangiroa

Famous French Polynesians: Marama Vahirua (footballer), Célestine Hitiura Vaite (author), Ella Koon (actress and singer)

Country Flag

Did You Know?

- French Polynesia is made up of 118 islands and atolls, spread over an area as large as Europe, but most of its land is just tiny dots in the Pacific Ocean.
- Bora Bora, often called the "Pearl of the Pacific," is famous for its stunning overwater bungalows and crystal-clear blue waters, making it a dream destination for many.
- Did you know the word "tattoo" comes from the Tahitian word "tatau"? Tattoos have been a significant part of Polynesian culture for thousands of years.
- The Marquesas Islands are home to ancient stone tiki statues, mysterious remnants of early Polynesian civilization, similar to the famous moai of Easter Island.
- The Tuamotu Archipelago has some of the best diving spots in the world, thanks to its rich marine life, including sharks, rays, and countless fish species living around the coral reefs.
- Tahaa Island is often called the "Vanilla Island" because it produces 80% of French Polynesia's vanilla. The air there smells sweetly of vanilla!
- With little light pollution, the islands offer some of the clearest night skies, perfect for stargazing and spotting constellations.

Mount Otemanu in Bora Bora

Where in the world is French Polynesia ...

Tiare Tahiti Flower

National Animal: Sea Turtle

Word Scramble

1. LOAONG   _ _ _ _ _ _
2. TITIAH   _ _ _ _ _ _
3. ABOR ROBA   _ _ _ _ _ _ _ _
4. OSTIYEC SIASNLD   _ _ _ _ _ _ _ _ _ _ _ _ _ _
5. EEAETPP   _ _ _ _ _ _ _
6. MNOUT UEATNMO _ _ _ _ _ _ _ _ _ _ _
7. LGERPHAIACO   _ _ _ _ _ _ _ _ _ _
8. HRNECF YESLINAPO _ _ _ _ _ _ _ _ _ _ _ _ _ _ _
9. TATOTOS   _ _ _ _ _ _ _
10. SAE STETRLU _ _ _ _ _ _ _ _ _
11. IERAT ITATIH _ _ _ _ _ _ _ _ _ _ _
12. RAMOEO   _ _ _ _ _ _

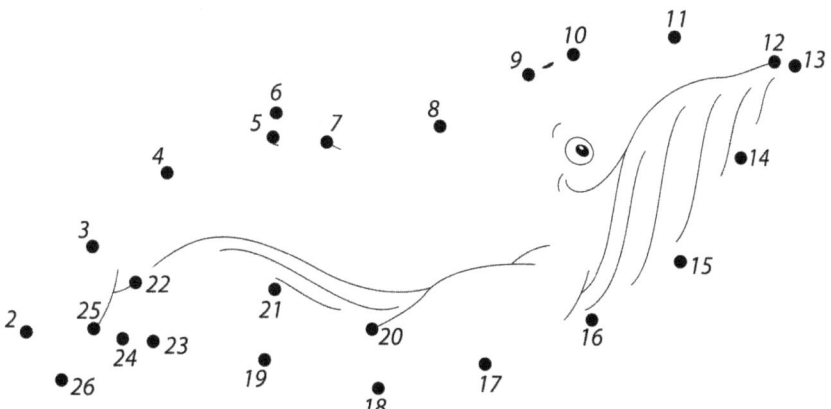

GUAM

Guam is a small island in the Pacific Ocean that is a territory of the United States. It's famous for its tropical beaches, coral reefs rich with marine life, and the intriguing Chamorro culture that calls this island home. Guam's history is fascinating, featuring ancient latte stones and historic sites from World War II. The island offers fun activities like snorkeling, hiking in the lush jungle, and exploring underwater caves. For the locals, or "Chamorros," celebrating their traditions and welcoming visitors with warm hospitality is a way of life.

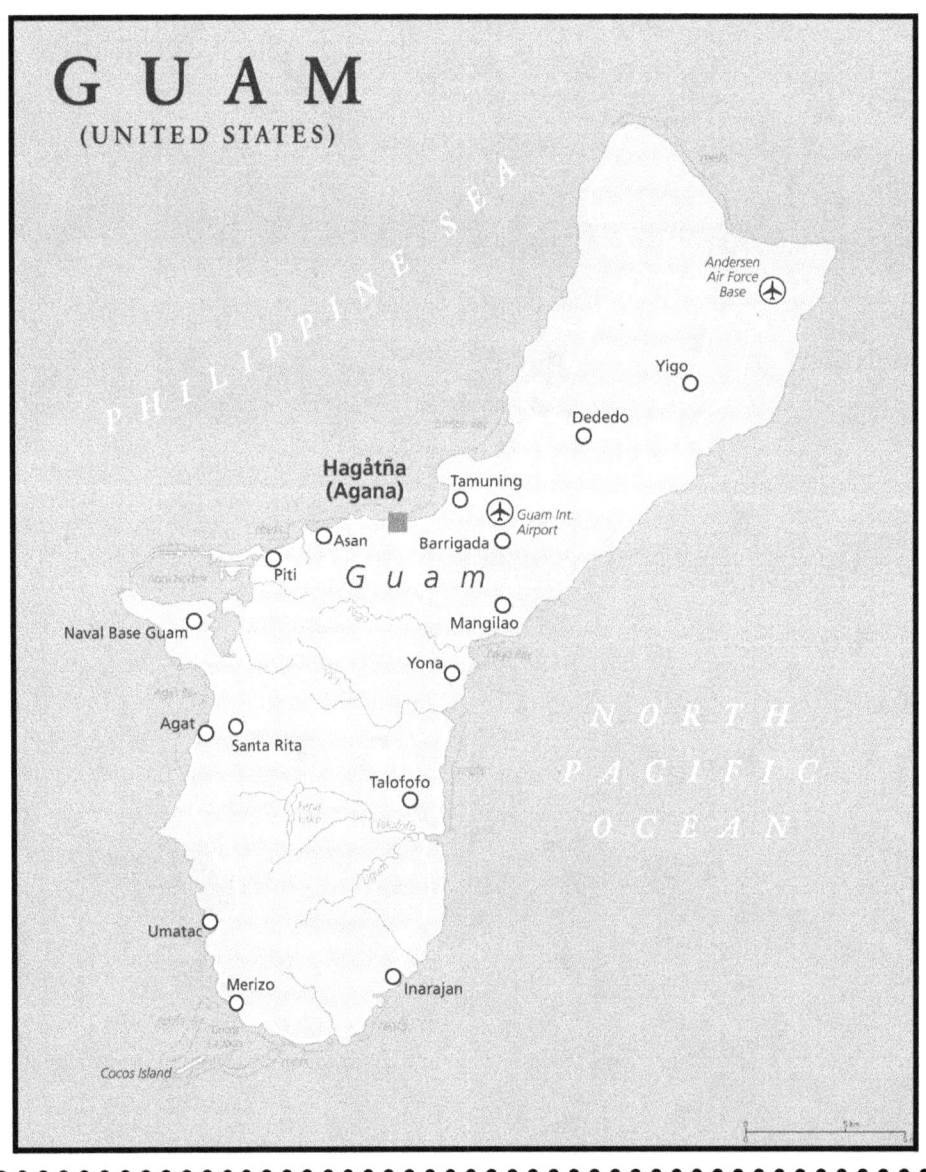

Facts About Guam

Capital:	Hagåtña
National Motto:	No official motto
Area:	212 square miles (549 square kilometers)
Major Cities:	Hagåtña, Dededo, Yigo
Population:	171,774
Bordering Countries:	Maritime boundaries with Northern Mariana Islands, Federated States of Micronesia
Languages:	English and Chamorro
Major Landmarks:	War in the Pacific National Historical Park, Tumon Bay, Latte Stone Park, Ritidian Point
Famous Guamanians:	Pia Mia (singer), Madeleine Bordallo (politician), Father Duenas (priest), Lou Leon Guerrero (governor)

Country Flag

Did You Know?

- **Super-sized Spiders:** Guam is home to enormous coconut crabs and orb-weaving spiders that can span the size of a dinner plate. Don't worry, they're more fascinating than scary!
- Guam has a significant World War II history, including the War in the Pacific National Historical Park, where you can visit old battle sites and memorials.
- **Two Sunsets in One Day:** Because of its proximity to the International Date Line, if you fly from Guam to Hawaii, you can technically experience two sunsets in the same day due to the time zone change.
- Guam has one of the highest per capita consumption rates of SPAM® in the world. It's a local favorite found in many dishes.
- **Underwater Mailbox:** Yes, you can actually send a waterproof postcard from an underwater mailbox located off the coast of Guam in one of its marine preserves.
- **Latte Stones:** Unique to Guam and the Marianas, latte stones are ancient megalithic structures that were used as foundation pillars for houses by the indigenous Chamorro people.

Latte Stones

Where in the world is Guam ...

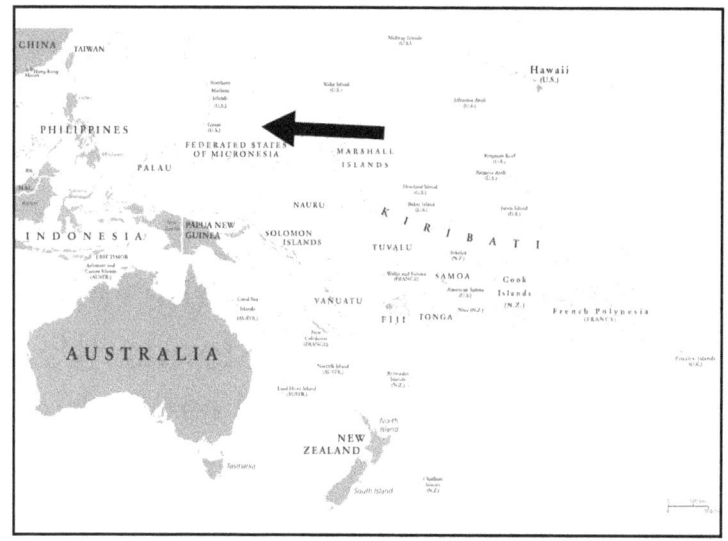

Guam quarter

Guam rail - endangered flightless bird

Word Search

CHAMORRO
CRABS
GUAM
HAGATNA
LATTE STONES
RAIL BIRD
SNORKELING
SPAM
SPIDERS
SUNSETS
TIME ZONE
UNITED STATES

```
L A T T E S T O N E S D D M G
K G W S X U S A O O D M F L O
L Z P E C S X F S K S F D P Q
C S Z T G U U Q O R P R K Q W
A H A A J U Q N E V I U W T V
X X Z T S N G D S B U G D I T
S V I S X N I N L E K N H M S
P U G D T P O I U N T G D E Z
A T E E S F A R I S C S A Z G
M R Q T U R A H K V I Q Q O S
X O S I R U K R T E S F A N B
S N C N B N I V L E L V X E A
E U C U T A A D O K E I C N R
R E A N T A G A H B J J N D C
G U A M O R R O M A H C D G Y
```

KIRIBATI

Kiribati is a unique country spread across the equator in the central Pacific Ocean, made up of 33 coral atolls and reef islands. It's known for its beautiful lagoons, diverse marine life, and extensive coral reefs, making it a paradise for diving and fishing. Kiribati has a rich cultural heritage, with music, dance, and handicrafts that reflect the islanders' connection to the sea and their environment. Despite its beauty, Kiribati is facing challenges due to rising sea levels, highlighting its role in global conversations about climate change. Life in Kiribati revolves around the community, the ocean, and respect for nature, offering a glimpse into a lifestyle deeply intertwined with the environment.

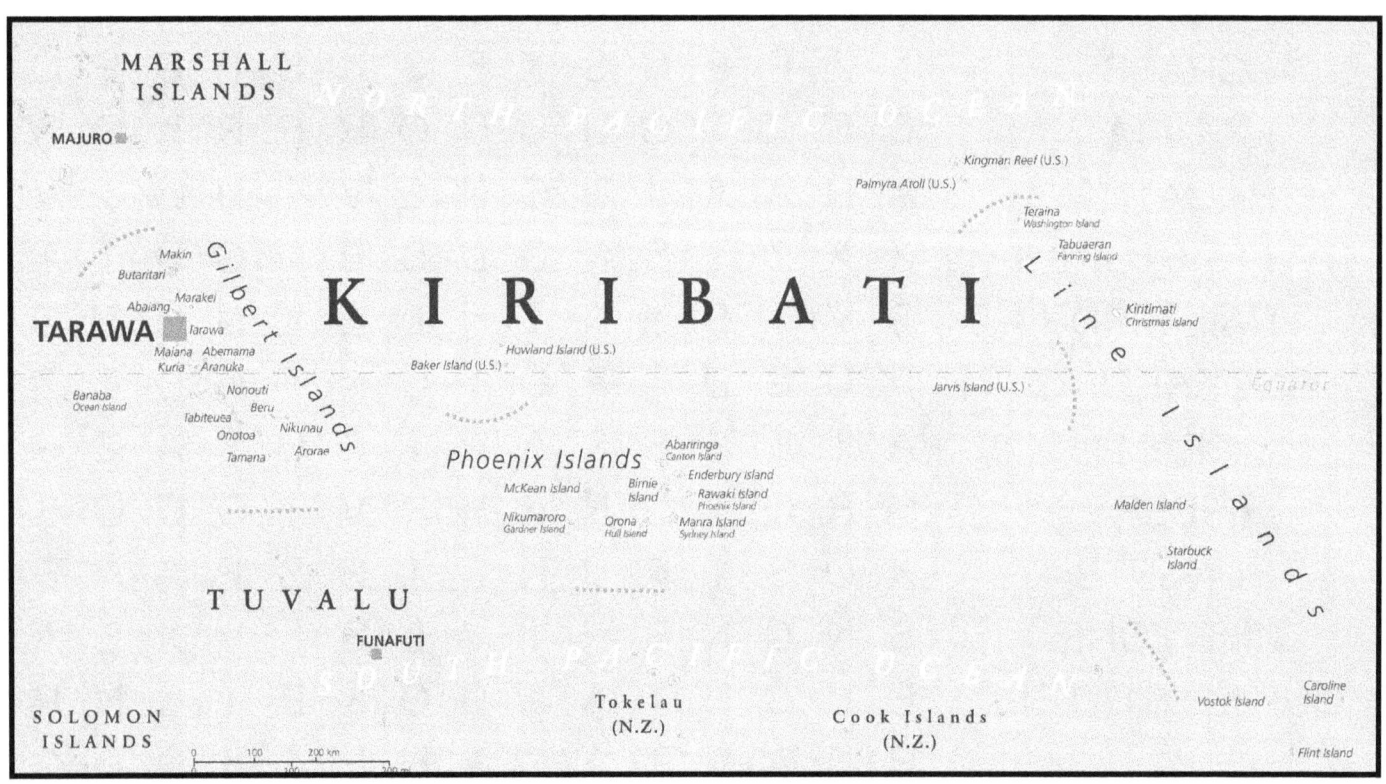

Facts About Kiribati

Capital: Tarawa
National Motto: Health, Peace, and Prosperity
Area: 313.1 square miles (811 square kilometers)
Major Cities: Tarawa, Betio Village, Bikenibeu
Population: 128,874
Bordering Countries: Cook Islands, Tokelau, French Polynesia
Language: Gilbertese (Kiribatese), English
Major Landmarks: Phoenix Islands Protected Area, Tarawa Atoll, Christmas Island, Equator and International Date Line Monuments
Famous Kiribatians: Anote Tong (politician), David Katoatau (weightlifter)

Country Flag

Did You Know?

- Kiribati is made up of 33 islands spread out over a huge area of the Pacific Ocean, but if you put all the land together, it's only about the size of New York City!
- Since Kiribati is one of the first countries to see the sunrise each day, it's like they live in the future. They were the first to welcome the year 2000!
- It rains a lot in Kiribati, but that doesn't stop the fun. Kids and adults alike enjoy dancing in the warm tropical rain.
- One of Kiribati's islands is called Christmas Island, but don't expect snow—it's the world's largest coral atoll and a haven for birds and crabs, not reindeer!
- Just like in Guam, you can send a postcard from an underwater mailbox in Kiribati. Talk about snail mail!
- The islands are famous for their coconut crabs, which are the largest land crabs in the world. They can crack open coconuts with their strong claws.
- Fishing is a big deal in Kiribati. The surrounding ocean is teeming with all sorts of fish, making it a great spot for fishing adventures.

Frigatebird

Where in the world is Kiribati ...

Maneaba traditional meeting house

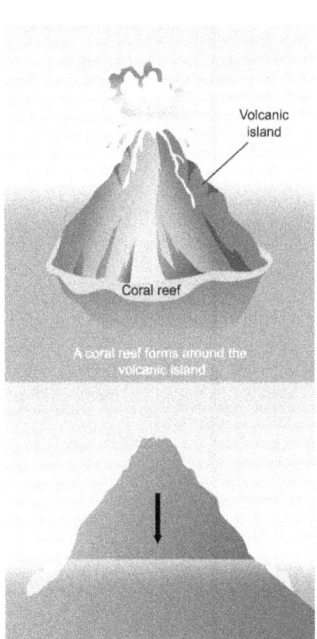

How a Coral Atoll Forms

1. It all starts with an underwater volcano erupting. Over time, the lava builds up and creates a volcanic island above the ocean surface.
2. Coral larvae attach to the edges of the volcanic island and start to grow. These tiny animals form a fringing reef around the island, creating a beautiful coral ecosystem.
3. Over millions of years, the volcanic island begins to sink and erode. This process is called subsidence.
4. As the island sinks, the coral reef continues to grow upward and outward. The reef becomes a barrier reef, with a lagoon forming between the reef and the remaining island.
5. Eventually, the volcanic island sinks completely below the ocean surface. What's left is a ring-shaped coral reef called an atoll, surrounding a central lagoon.
6. The atoll continues to thrive as long as conditions remain favorable for coral growth, providing a home for diverse marine life.

This process, taking millions of years, transforms a volcanic island into a vibrant and beautiful coral atoll.

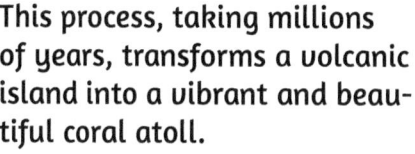

MARSHALL ISLANDS

The Marshall Islands are a group of atolls and islands in the central Pacific Ocean, known for their stunning blue lagoons and vibrant coral reefs. This country is a haven for divers and snorkelers, offering underwater exploration of shipwrecks from World War II and an abundance of marine life. The Marshallese culture is rich with navigation and canoeing traditions, showcasing the islanders' deep connection to the sea. The Marshall Islands also played a significant role in nuclear testing during the mid-20th century, which has shaped much of its recent history and efforts toward peace and environmental preservation. Community life here emphasizes sharing, cooperation, and a strong bond with nature.

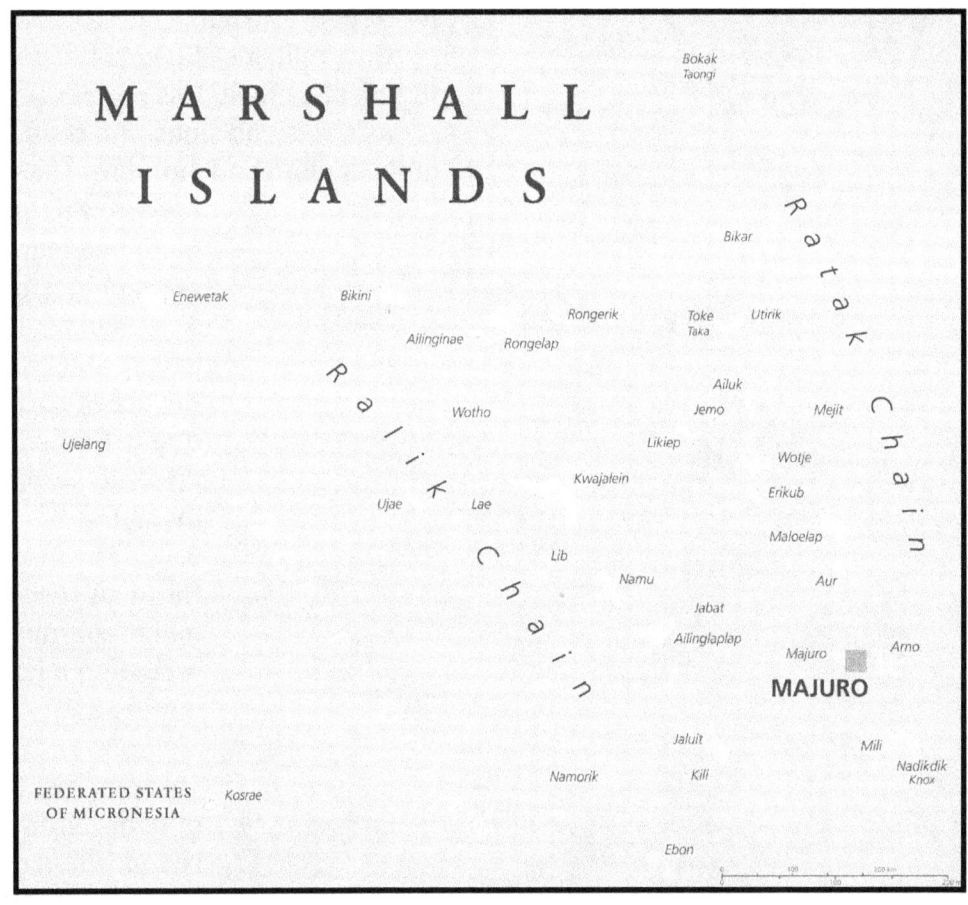

Facts About Marshall Islands

Capital:	Majuro
National Motto:	Accomplishment/Achievement through Joint Effort
Area:	69.88 square miles (181 square kilometers)
Major Cities:	Majuro, Ebaye, Arno
Population:	42,050
Bordering Countries:	Maritime borders with the Federated States of Micronesia, Kiribati, and Nauru
Languages:	Marshallese, English
Major Landmarks:	Bikini Atoll, Majuro Atoll, Arno Atoll
Famous Marshallese:	Amata Kabua (president), Tony de Brum (politician), Kathy Jetnil-Kijiner (poet)

Country Flag

Did You Know?

- The Marshall Islands are made up of over 1,000 tiny islands and islets grouped into 29 atolls, which are like necklace-shaped coral reefs. Imagine exploring a new island every day!
- The Bikini Atoll here is famous for its underwater shipwrecks from World War II. Divers can explore sunken battleships and submarines, creating an underwater museum.
- The Kwajalein Atoll is home to one of the world's largest space and missile testing facilities. It's like a launch pad to the stars right from the middle of the ocean.
- Believe it or not, basketball is super popular in the Marshall Islands. Kids and adults play it everywhere, from small village courts to bigger arenas.
- Some beaches here have bioluminescent plankton that glow in the dark. Walking along the shore at night is like stepping on stars.
- Coconuts are not just for eating here; the Marshall Islands use them for "copra" (dried coconut meat) to make coconut oil and other products.

Spinner Dolphin

Where in the world are Marshall Islands ...

Traditional canoes known as Proas

Traditional Marshallese stick chart used for navigation

Crossword Puzzle

Across

3. Atoll famous for its shipwrecks (6)
4. Common natural material used in Marshallese handicrafts (7)
5. Traditional boat used in Marshall Islands (5)
7. Main source of protein in Marshall Islands diet (4)
8. Capital of the Marshall Islands (6)
10. Popular sport in Marshall Islands (10)

Down

1. Divers can explore these World War II relics (10)
2. The Marshall Islands are part of this larger island group (10)
6. Type of coral formation surrounding a lagoon (5)
9. Marshall Islands were once under the control of this country (3)

NAURU

Nauru is one of the smallest countries in the world, located in the Pacific Ocean. It's an island known for its phosphate deposits, which have significantly influenced its economy and environment. Nauru has no rivers or streams, so fresh water is precious here. The island's history includes periods of significant wealth and environmental challenges due to intensive phosphate mining. Despite its small size, Nauru boasts a vibrant community with traditions and culture that reflect its Micronesian and Polynesian heritage. Sports, especially weightlifting and Australian rules football, are popular among its residents.

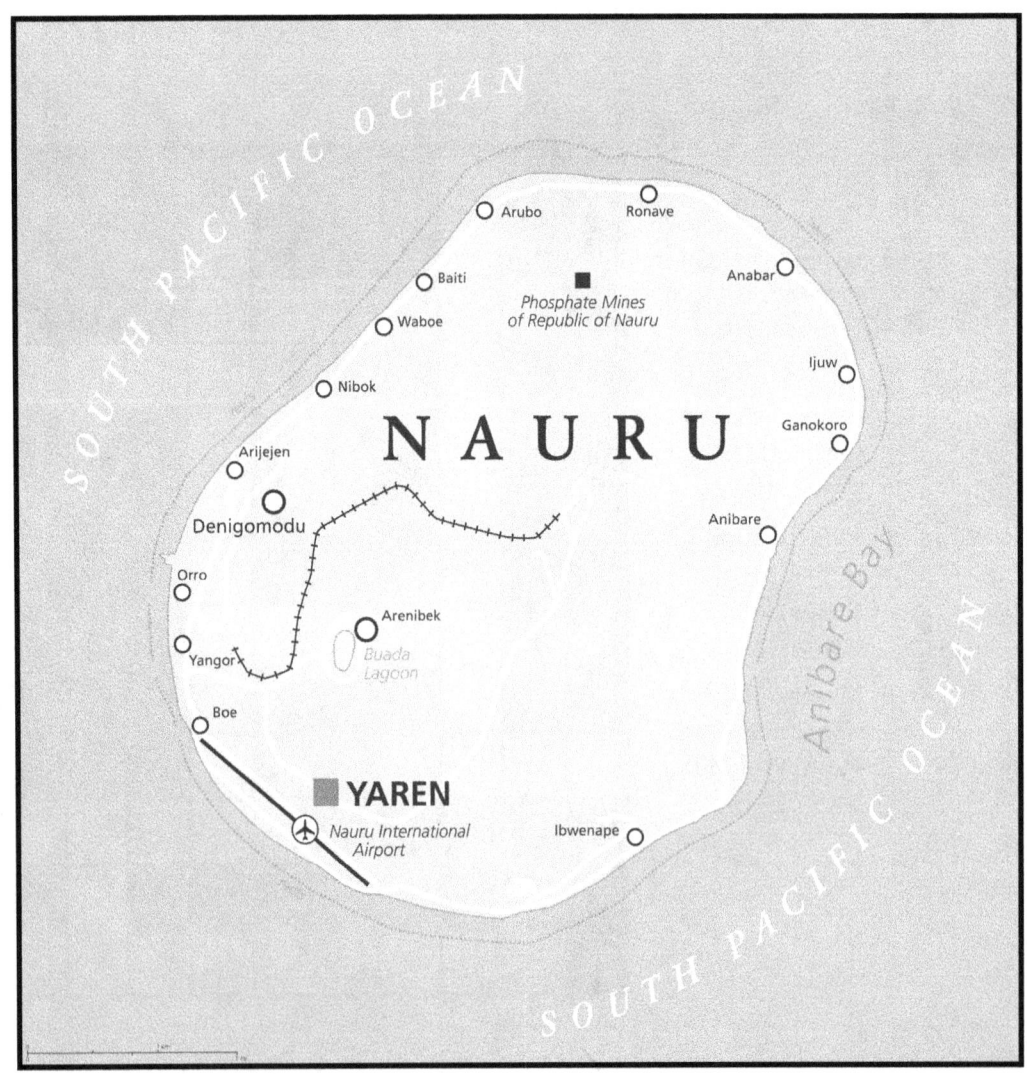

Facts About Nauru

Capital: Yaren
National Motto: God's Will First
Area: 8.1 square miles (21 square kilometers)
Major Cities: Yaren
Population: 12,511
Bordering Countries: Maritime borders with Marshall Islands, Federated States of Micronesia, Kiribati, Papua New Guinea, Solomon Islands
Language: Nauruan
Major Landmarks: Command Ridge, Anibare Bay, Buada Lagoon
Famous Nauruans: Hammer DeRoburt (president), Bernard Dowiyogo (president), Marcus Stephen (weightlifter)

Country Flag

Did You Know?

- Nauru is one of the smallest countries in the world. It's so small you can drive around the entire island in less than an hour!
- Despite its size, Nauru is a birdwatcher's dream. You can spot lots of exotic birds, making it seem like a huge, open-air aviary.
- Nauru is sitting on tons of phosphate, a mineral used to make things like fertilizer.
- People in Nauru love weightlifting. They're so good at it that they often compete in international competitions, lifting many times their own body weight.
- The entire island is the top of an ancient coral reef pushed up by the ocean floor.
- Folks in Nauru are big fans of Australian Rules Football. They play and watch it with lots of enthusiasm.

Coat of Arms

Where in the world is Nauru ...

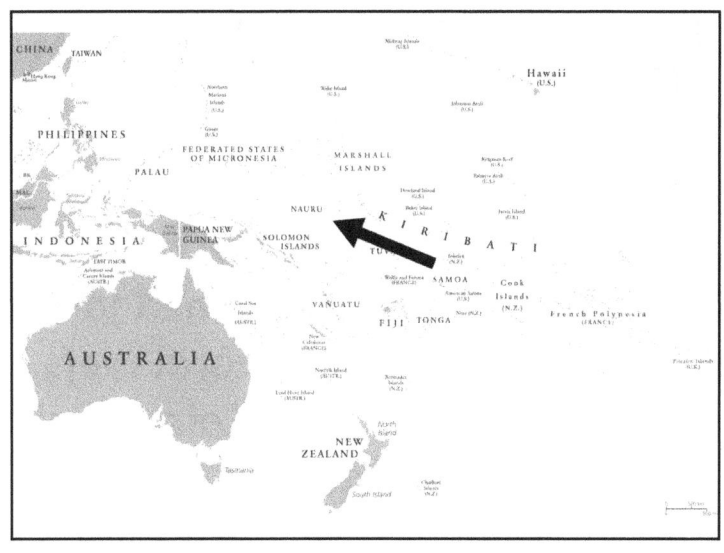

Nauruan weightlifter

Calophyllum

Maze
Help the bird find its nest

NEW CALEDONIA

New Caledonia is a French territory located in the South Pacific, known for its stunning lagoon, which is one of the largest in the world and a UNESCO World Heritage site. The region is famed for its rich biodiversity, both on land and in the surrounding coral reefs, making it a paradise for nature lovers and divers. New Caledonia's unique blend of Melanesian culture and French influence is evident in its food, language, and traditions. The capital, Nouméa, offers a mix of beautiful beaches, colonial architecture, and vibrant markets. The territory also has a strong commitment to protecting its environment, including efforts to preserve its native species and habitats.

Facts About New Caledonia

Capital: Nouméa
National Motto: Liberty, Equality, Fraternity
Area: 18,575.5 square kilometres (7,172 square miles)
Major Cities: Nouméa, Le Mont-Dore, Dumbéa and Païta
Population: 269,220
Bordering Countries: Maritime borders with Australia, Fiji, Papua New Guinea, Solomon Islands, and Vanuatu
Language: French
Major Landmarks: Great Barrier Reef of New Caledonia, Heart of Voh, Isle of Pines
Famous New Caledonians: Christian Karembeu (footballer), Roch Wamytan (politician), Valérie Ghibaudo (windsurfer)

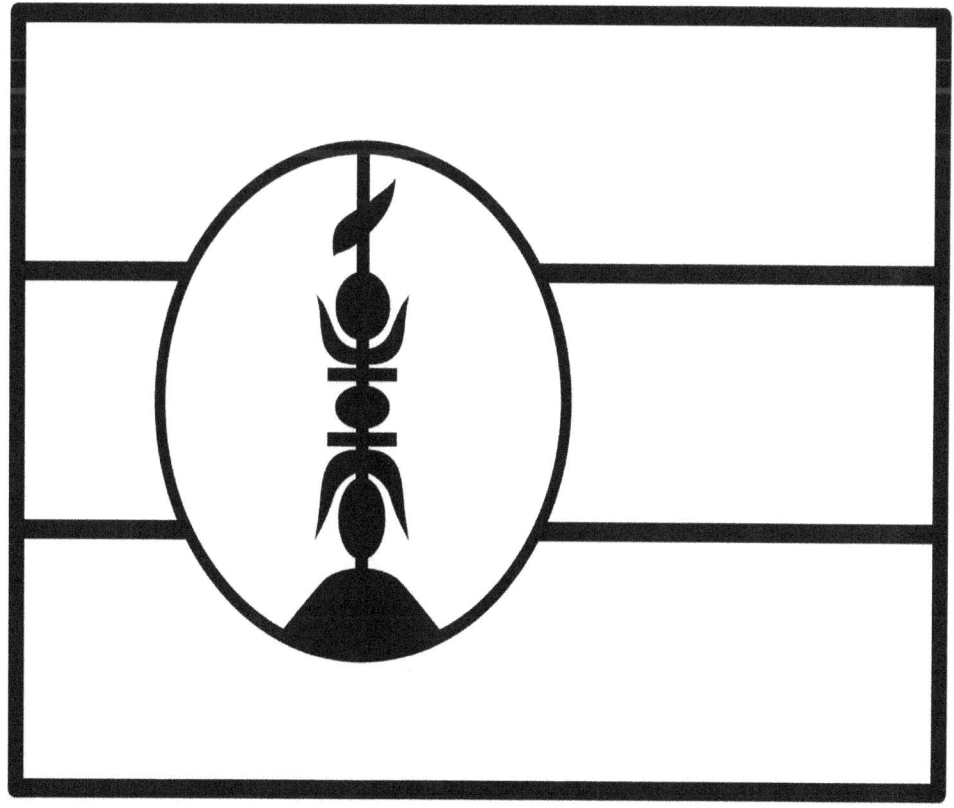

Country Flag

Did You Know?

- New Caledonia has one of the world's largest nickel deposits. It's like the island is sitting on a giant piggy bank!
- The surrounding coral reef forms a lagoon around New Caledonia, making it the second-largest barrier reef in the world.
- There's an island called "Heart Island" (Île des Pins) because it's shaped like a heart.
- The indigenous people of New Caledonia are called the Kanak, and they have rich traditions and a strong connection to the land.
- New Caledonia is home to the kagu, a bird that looks like it's wearing fluffy gray pants. It's found nowhere else in the world!
- Blue River Park: This park isn't just green; it has a Blue River, where the water sometimes looks bright blue due to the minerals in the soil.
- Even though it's a small place, over 28 different languages are spoken in New Caledonia.

Where in the world is New Caledonia ...

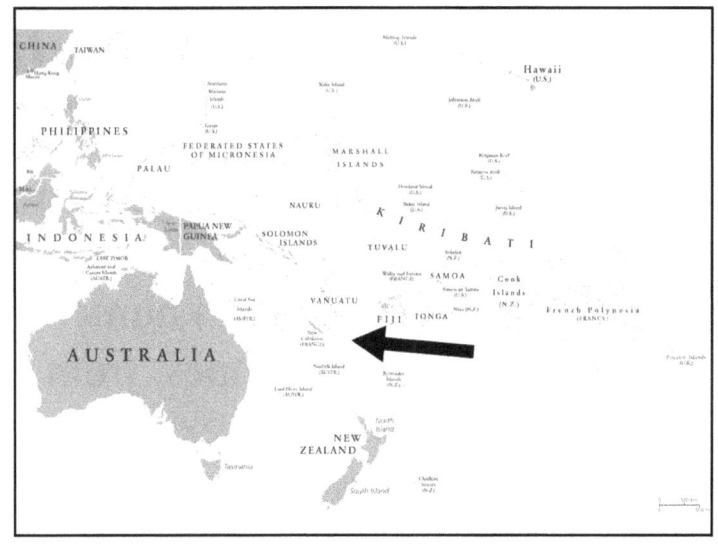

Emblem of New Caledonia

Kagu Bird

BLUE RIVER
CALDEDONIA
ENVIRONMENT
FRANCE
HEART ISLAND
KAGU BIRD
KANAK
LAGOONS
NICKEL
NOUMEA
OCEAN
SOUTH PACIFIC

Word Search

E	M	C	N	I	C	K	E	L	V	D	O	C	T	D
I	J	I	T	E	E	F	L	E	R	P	Y	I	S	V
M	B	F	D	C	N	Z	R	I	K	A	N	A	K	W
O	L	I	E	I	S	V	B	A	A	T	F	G	V	A
P	U	C	F	H	P	U	I	P	N	E	H	S	E	N
Q	E	A	E	D	G	D	G	R	E	C	N	F	C	O
L	R	P	R	A	B	Z	E	U	O	O	E	Y	V	U
N	I	H	K	F	V	O	B	C	O	N	C	V	M	M
A	V	T	R	N	J	G	W	G	S	I	M	V	L	E
E	E	U	X	G	E	G	A	A	B	M	M	E	B	A
C	R	O	O	M	M	L	W	C	E	M	B	V	N	F
O	H	S	D	N	A	L	S	I	T	R	A	E	H	T
C	A	L	D	E	D	O	N	I	A	G	Z	K	P	B
T	T	J	W	G	K	Z	E	V	Y	T	E	P	P	L
E	J	L	H	R	N	U	H	A	I	P	D	S	M	R

NEW ZEALAND

New Zealand, also known as Aotearoa in the Maori language, is a country in the southwestern Pacific Ocean consisting of two main islands, the North Island and the South Island, along with numerous smaller islands. It's famous for its stunning landscapes, from towering mountains and misty fjords to rolling hills and expansive beaches. New Zealand is a paradise for outdoor enthusiasts, offering activities like hiking, skiing, and bungee jumping. The country has a rich cultural heritage, with the indigenous Maori people's traditions and legends playing a significant role in everyday life. New Zealand is also known for its commitment to environmental conservation, protecting its unique wildlife and natural areas.

Facts About New Zealand

Capital: Wellington
National Motto: No official motto, formerly Onward
Area: 103,750 square miles (268,710 square kilometers)
Major Cities: Auckland, Wellington, Christchurch, Hamilton
Population: 5.123 million
Bordering Countries: Maritime borders with American Samoa, Australia, Fiji, French Polynesia, Kiribati, Samoa, and Tonga
Language: English
Major Landmarks: Milford Sound, Waitomo Glowworm Caves, Sky Tower
Famous New Zealanders: Edmund Hillary (explorer), Peter Jackson (filmmaker), Lorde (singer)

Country Flag

Did You Know?

- New Zealand has one of the longest place names in the world. Try saying this fast: "Taumatawhakatangihangakoauauotamateaturipukakapikimaungahoronukupokaiwhenuakitnatahu"!
- Waitomo Caves are home to thousands of glowworms that light up the cave ceilings like stars in the night sky.
- The first commercial bungee jump started in Queenstown, New Zealand.
- More Sheep Than People: There are about six sheep for every person in New Zealand.
- New Zealand sits on the Pacific Ring of Fire, so it has lots of geothermal wonders like geysers and hot springs.
- Just like the famous Northern Lights, New Zealand has its own version called the Southern Lights or Aurora Australis.
- In New Zealand, people drive on the left side of the road.
- World's Steepest Street: Baldwin Street in Dunedin was once recognized as the world's steepest residential street.
- The Kiwi bird, New Zealand's national symbol, is so unique that it's sometimes called a "dinosaur bird." It has tiny wings but can't fly, and its nostrils are at the tip of its beak.

Coat of arms

Where in the world is New Zealand ...

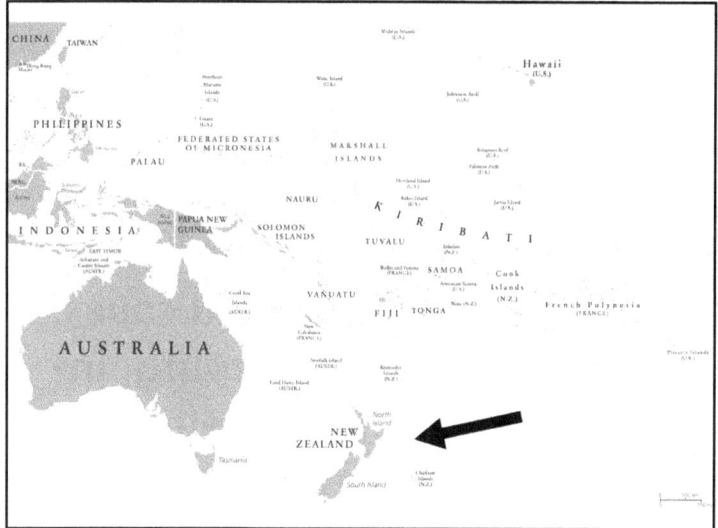

**National Bird:
Kiwi Bird**

**National Plant:
Silver fern**

- A flightless bird with a long beak, known for its nocturnal habits and iconic status as a national symbol.

- One of the smallest and rarest dolphins in the world, identifiable by its rounded dorsal fin.

- A reptile that resembles a lizard but belongs to a unique lineage; often referred to as a "living fossil."

- A large, nocturnal, flightless parrot known for its green feathers and critically endangered status.

- The smallest penguin species in the world, known for its blue feathers and coastal habitat.

- A domesticated animal known for its wool. New Zealand has more of this animal than people, making them a significant part of the landscape and economy.

Animal Match

New Zealand is home to many unique animals. Read each description and look for clues about the animal's appearance, behavior, or special features. Draw a line from each animal picture to the matching description.

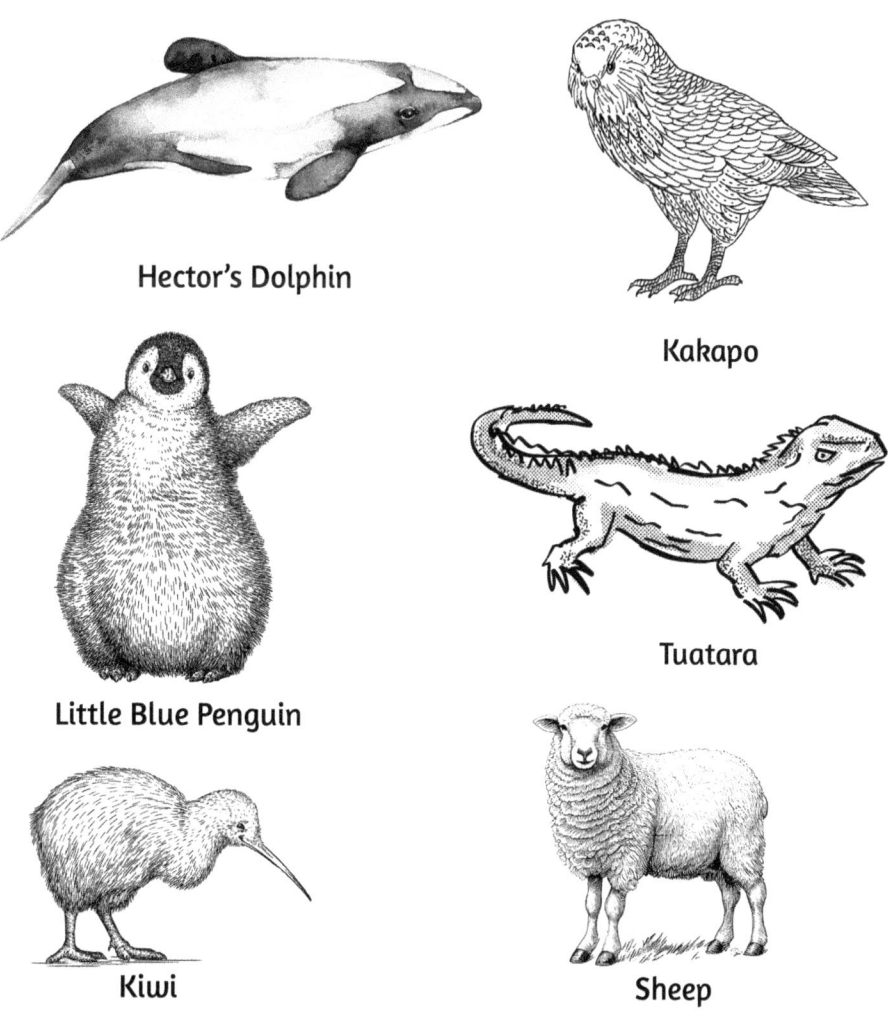

NIUE

Niue is a small island nation in the South Pacific Ocean, often referred to as "The Rock" because of its limestone cliffs and caves. Despite its compact size, Niue is packed with natural beauty, including crystal-clear waters, coral reefs perfect for snorkeling and diving, and lush rainforests. It's one of the world's largest raised coral atolls and is known for its commitment to preserving its environment, being the first country to become a Dark Sky Nation, ideal for stargazing. Niue has a close-knit community with a rich Polynesian culture, where traditional customs are still celebrated. The island offers a peaceful retreat with warm, welcoming locals and untouched landscapes, making it a unique destination for travelers seeking tranquility and adventure in nature.

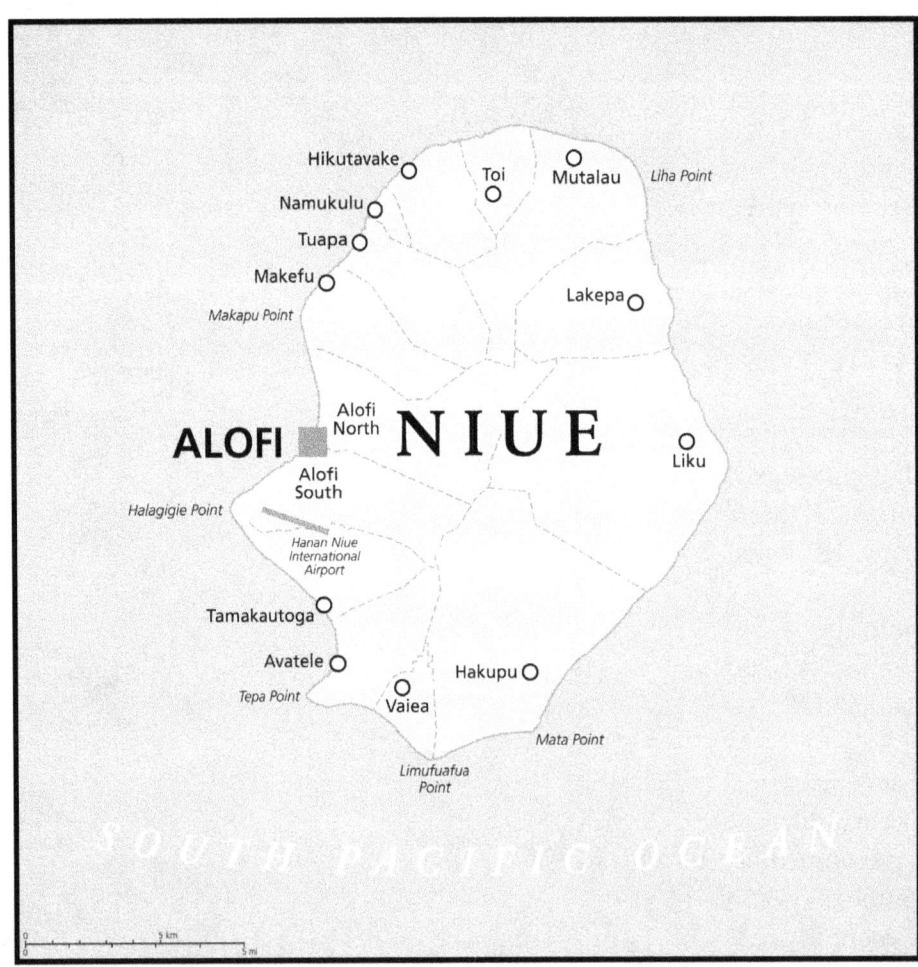

Facts About Niue

Capital:	Alofi
National Motto:	God, Niue Eternally
Area:	261.46 square kilometres (100.95 sq mi)
Major Villages:	Alofi, Hakupu, Avatele
Population:	1,689
Bordering Countries:	Maritime borders with Tonga, Samoa, and Cook Islands
Languages:	English, Niuean
Major Landmarks:	Togo Chasm, Hikutavake Pools, Liku Sea Track and Cave
Famous Niueans:	Sir Robert Rex (Premier), Patricia O'Brien (diplomat), John Pule (artist)

Country Flag

Did You Know?

- Niue is one of the smallest countries on Earth. Imagine a whole country where everyone could know your name!
- Niue is one of the world's largest raised coral atolls.
- Niue uses New Zealand dollars, but they also have their own cool coins with Star Wars and Disney characters on them.
- The water around Niue is so clear you can see up to 80 meters deep.
- Niue has a huge natural swimming pool called Limu Pools, with crystal clear water.
- Despite its remote location, Niue was the first country to offer free Wi-Fi to everyone on the island. You can post selfies from almost anywhere!
- Every year, humpback whales visit Niue's waters to give birth, making it a perfect spot for whale watching right from the shore.

National flower: Fiti Pua

Where in the world is Niue ...

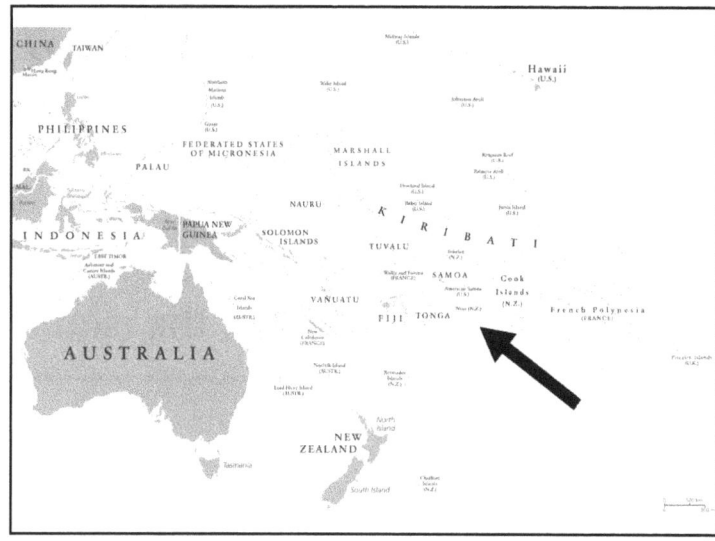

Humpback whale

Crossword Puzzle

Across

1. Animal that visits Niue every year (6)
3. A natural swimming pool in Niue (4,5)
5. National flower of Niue (4,3)
7. Niue is known as "The _____" (4)
9. Traditional house style in Niue (4)
10. Main underwater activity for tourists in Niue (6)

Down

2. Capital of Niue (5)
4. A popular nightime activity in Niue (10)
6. Niue is located in this ocean region (9)
8. Fruit grown in Niue (7)

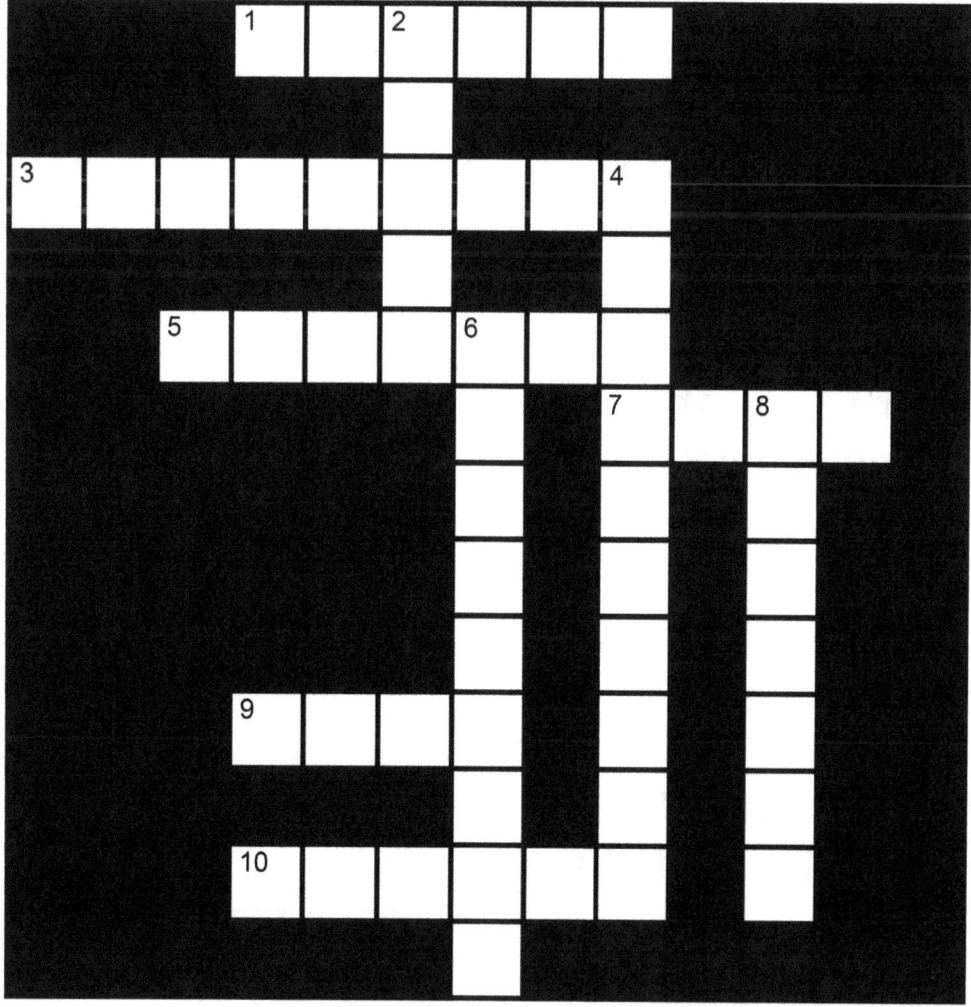

NORFOLK ISLAND

Norfolk Island is a small Australian external territory located in the Pacific Ocean between Australia, New Zealand, and New Caledonia. Known for its rugged coastline, pine trees, and rich history, the island was once a convict penal colony. Today, Norfolk Island offers a unique blend of breathtaking natural beauty, historical sites, and a distinct culture that includes influences from the Bounty Mutineers, who settled the island in the 19th century. Visitors can explore the island's lush national parks, enjoy bird watching, dive into crystal-clear waters, or learn about the island's intriguing past at the Kingston and Arthur's Vale Historic Area. The island community, with its own language and customs, warmly welcomes travelers to discover its hidden treasures.

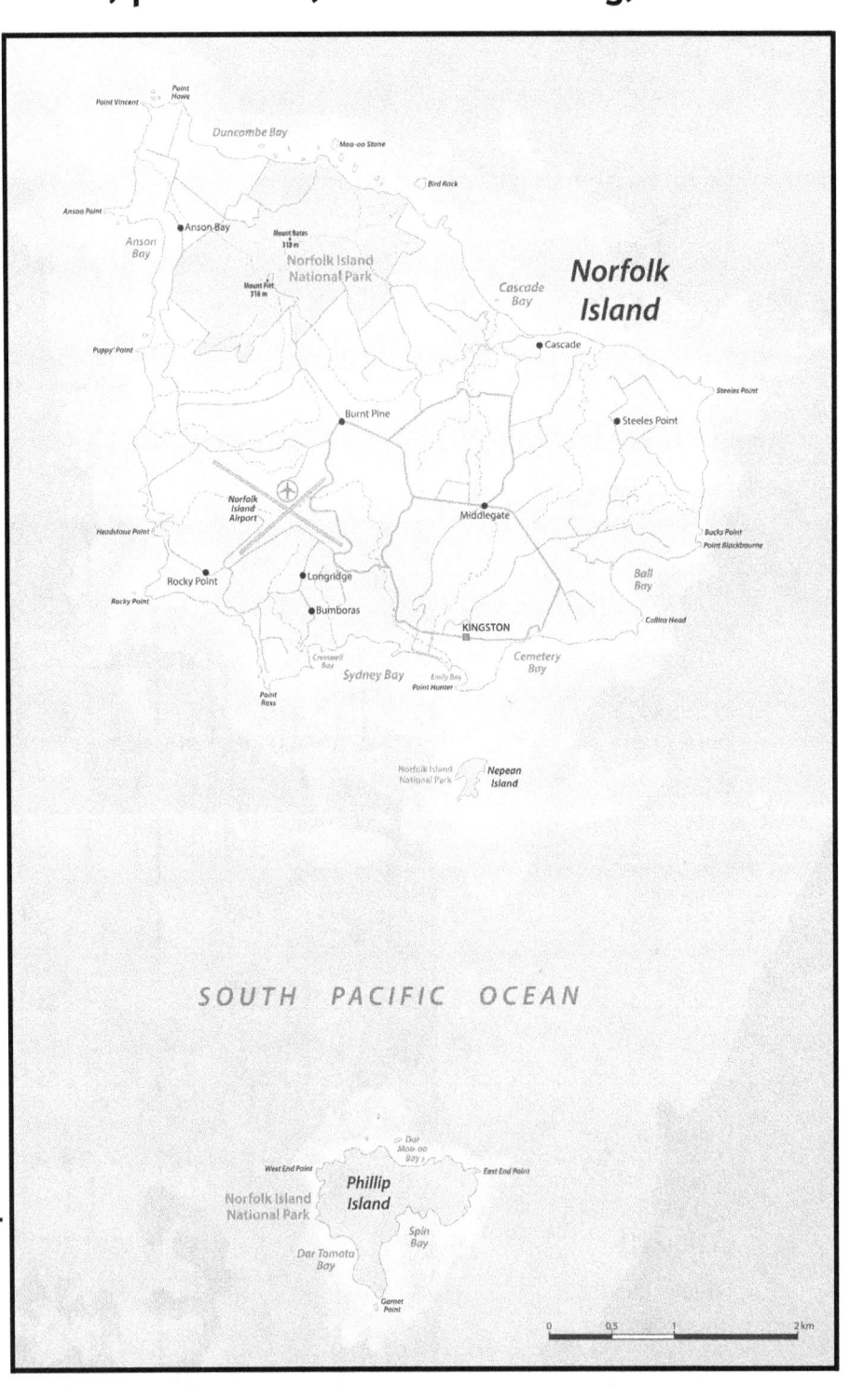

Facts About Norfolk Island

Capital: Kingston
National Motto: Inasmuch
Area: 13.3 square miles (34.6 square kilometers)
Major Cities: Kingston, Burnt Pine
Population: 2,188
Bordering Countries: Australia, New Zealand, and New Caledonia
Languages: English and Norfuk
Major Landmarks: Kingston and Arthur's Vale Historic Area (KAVHA), Captain Cook Monument, Norfolk Island National Park, The Old Watermill
Famous Norfolk Islanders: Colleen McCullough (author), Rebecca Christian (conservationist), Sir John Call (politician)

Country Flag

Did You Know?

- Norfolk Island may be small, but it was once a harsh penal colony. Today, it's a peaceful place with a fascinating history to explore.
- Locals speak Norf'k, a unique language that blends old English and Tahitian.
- Norfolk Island is home to some of the world's tallest tree ferns. Walking among them is like wandering through a prehistoric forest.
- The island is a haven for rare birds, including the endangered Norfolk Island parakeet.
- With minimal light pollution, the stars and Milky Way shine brightly at night.
- Norfolk Island pines are famous worldwide. Originally used as ship masts during the 18th and 19th centuries, these trees are now an iconic symbol of the island.
- The Norfolk Island Golf Course is set within the Kingston and Arthur's Vale Historic Area, allowing you to play among ruins of the penal colony.
- Emily Bay is a protected coral reef lagoon with crystal clear water, perfect for snorkeling and swimming.

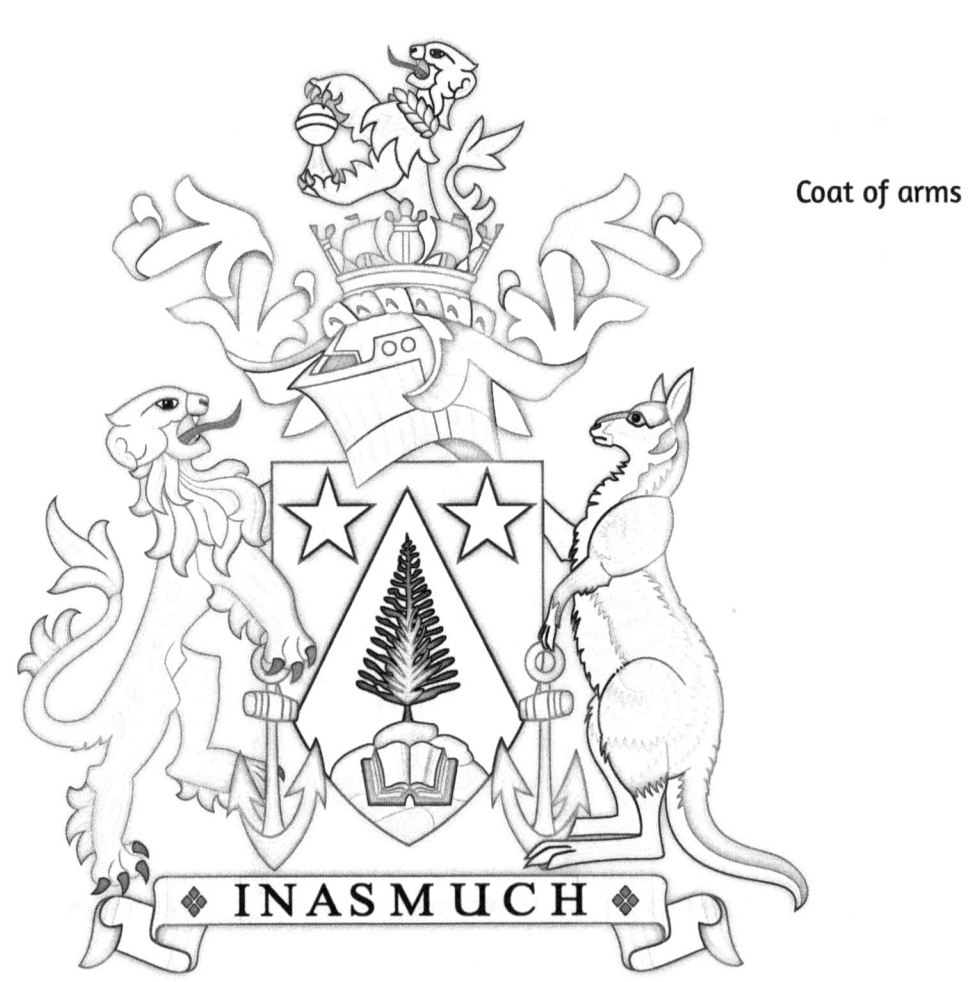

Coat of arms

Where in the world is Norfolk Island ...

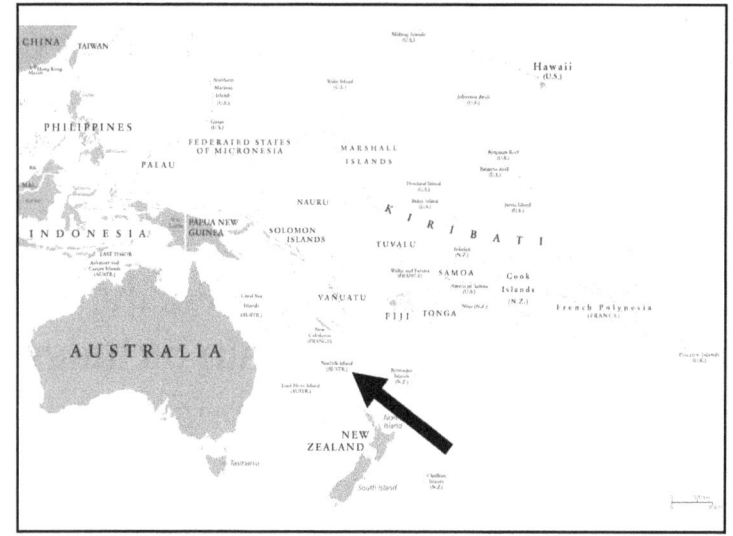

Green Parrot

Norfolk Island Pine trees

Maze Game
Find your way from Point Vincent in the north to Point Hunter in the south.

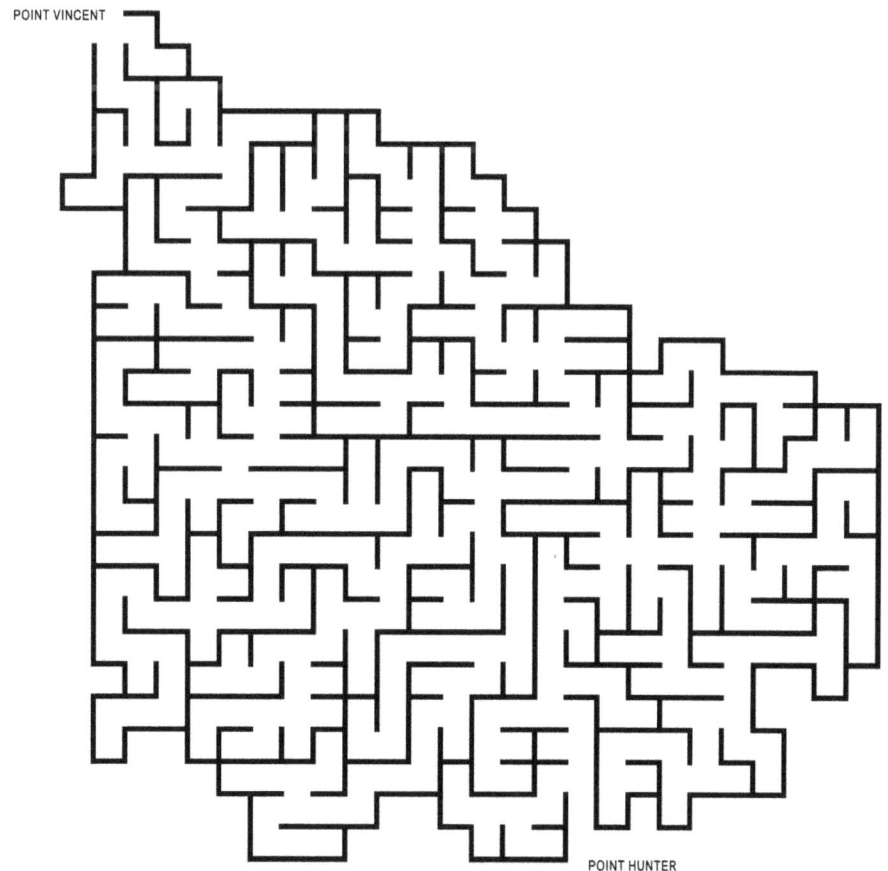

NORTHERN MARIANA ISLANDS

The Northern Mariana Islands, a group of islands in the Pacific Ocean, are a commonwealth of the United States. This chain includes 14 islands, with Saipan, Tinian, and Rota being the most populated and visited. Known for their stunning beaches, crystal-clear waters, and historical World War II sites, these islands offer a unique blend of natural beauty and history. The indigenous Chamorro and Carolinian cultures are vibrant and celebrated through music, dance, and festivals. The islands are also a paradise for outdoor activities, including diving in the Grotto, a limestone cave underwater, hiking to Mount Tapochau, Saipan's highest point, and exploring ancient latte stone sites. The Northern Mariana Islands are tranquil and picturesque with warm hospitality.

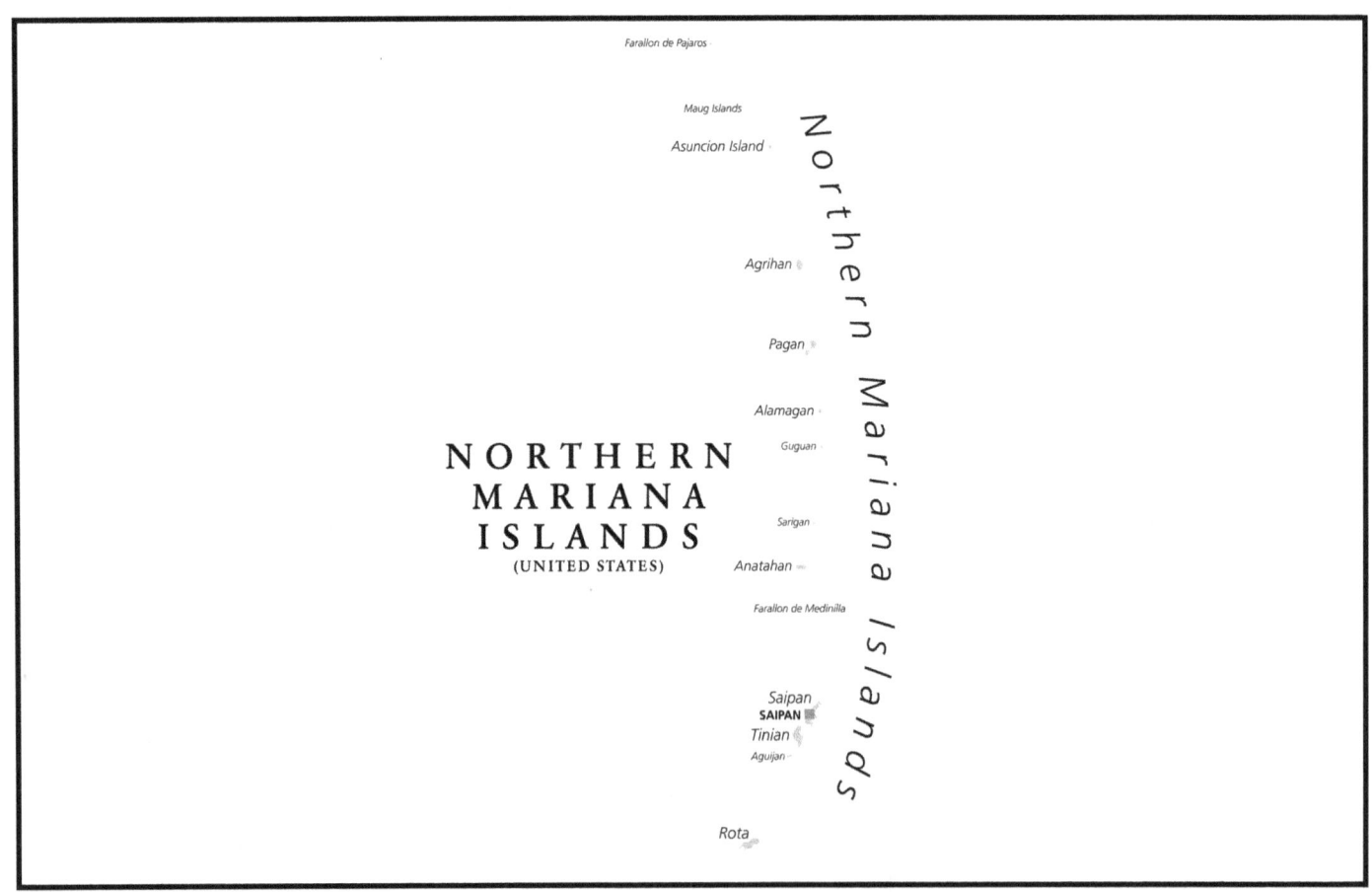

Facts About Northern Mariana Islands

Capital: Saipan
National Motto: No official motto
Area: 183.5 square miles (475.26 square kilometers)
Major Cities: Saipan, San Jose
Population: 49,551
Bordering Countries: Maritime borders with Guam, Micronesia
Languages: English and Chamorro
Major Landmarks: American Memorial Park, Grotto, Managaha Island, Mount Tapochau, Bird Island
Famous Northern Marianans: Kurt Barnes (golfer), Lori Phillips (opera singer), Frank "The Crank" Camacho (martial artist), Tyce Mister (football player)

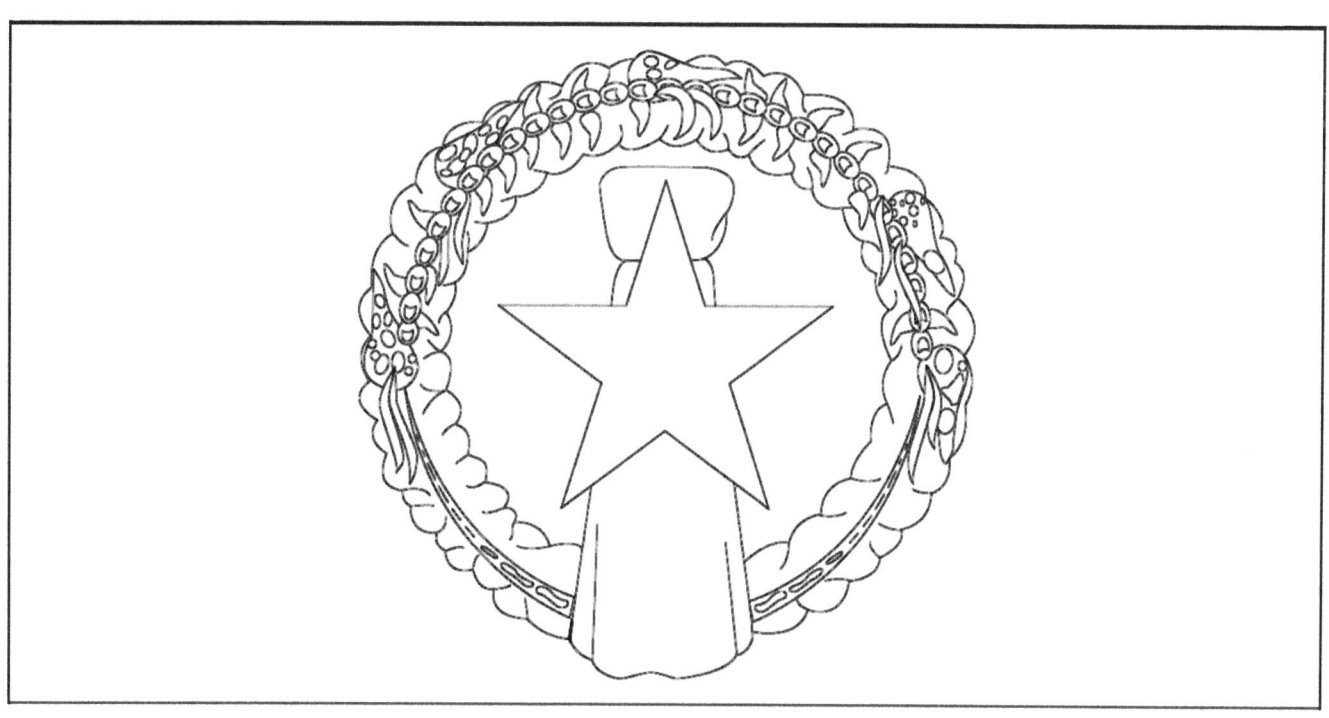

Country Flag

Did You Know?

- The Northern Mariana Islands have shipwrecks and airplanes from World War II under the sea.
- The Managaha Island lagoon's water is so clear, it feels like swimming among the stars during the day.
- In the spring, the islands are covered in bright red flame trees.
- The Grotto on Saipan is a natural limestone cave that's a swimming hole connected to the ocean.
- Mount Tapochau: The highest point offers views where you can see the whole island of Saipan.
- The Last Command Post: A historical landmark on Saipan, this bunker was the Japanese headquarters during WWII.
- A natural reserve off the coast of Saipan, Forbidden Island offers hiking trails, wildlife viewing, and snorkeling in its surrounding marine sanctuary.
- Bird Island Sanctuary is a small islet off Saipan that's a sanctuary for birds and marine life, accessible by kayak.

National bird: Mariana fruit dove

Where in the world are Northern Mariana Islands ...

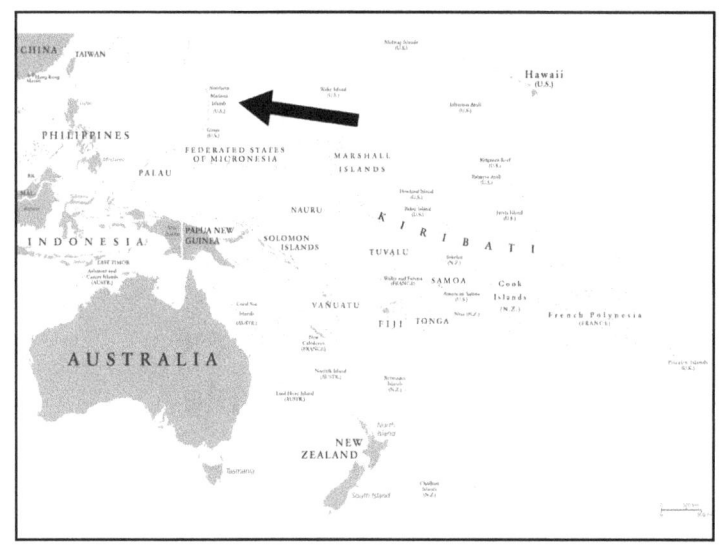

National flower: Plumeria

Word Search

BEACHES
CAROLINIAN
CHAMORRO
FRUIT DOVE
GROTTO
LIMESTONE
PLUMERIA
ROTA
SAIPAN
SHIPWRECKS
TAPOCHAU
TINIAN

```
N O G L X U C B D D I B P V H
P T I R N I E E Q W F K N Q C
C T Y C T V W D S N N I D S G
Z O L N A I N I L O R A C K N
L R G I C F O C R C D K N C N
T G U C M H N Y Q R O T A E B
A C O N M E A Y D H N C M R V
P W K U Z A S M H E W A I W D
O G F O X K S T O G I H Z P S
C L Q A Z E A Q O R E V G I A
H B S N H V D D E N R S J H I
A W W C Z F A M F E E O N S P
U M A T G V U M N A I N I T A
S E T V T L D L X H Z G N N N
B R E I P O F R U I T D O V E
```

PALAU

Palau is a tropical paradise located in the western Pacific Ocean, composed of around 340 islands. It's famous for its extraordinary marine life, pristine beaches, and the remarkable Rock Islands, which are UNESCO World Heritage sites. Palau offers some of the world's best diving spots, including Jellyfish Lake, where swimmers can float among millions of harmless jellyfish. The islands have a rich cultural heritage, with traditional customs and practices still a significant part of Palauan life. Visitors can explore dense jungles, kayak through mangroves, or learn about Palau's history at ancient stone monoliths and WWII sites. Palau is dedicated to conservation, creating the first shark sanctuary and emphasizing eco-friendly tourism.

Facts About Palau

Capital: Ngerulmud
National Motto: Rainbow's End
Area: 177.2 square miles (459 square kilometers)
Major Cities: Koror
Population: 18,055
Bordering Countries: Maritime borders with Micronesia, Indonesia, Philippines
Languages: Palauan, English
Major Landmarks: Rock Islands, Jellyfish Lake, Ngardmau Waterfall, Badrulchau Stone Monoliths
Famous Palauans: Tommy Remengesau (politician), Lazarus Salii (politician), Ymesei O. Ezekiel (poet), Ngeribongel Uriam (athlete)

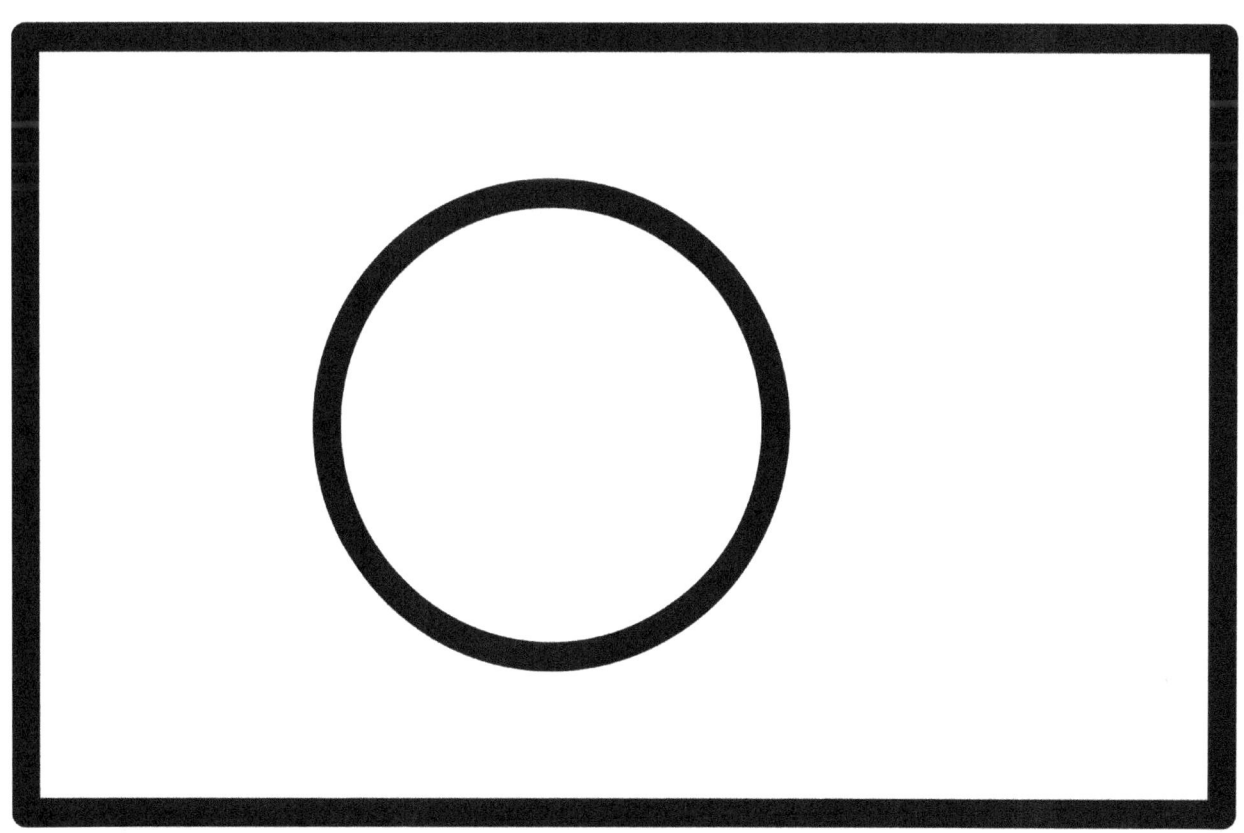

Country Flag

Did You Know?

- Imagine swimming with millions of jellyfish that don't sting! Palau's Jellyfish Lake is one of the few places in the world where you can do just that.
- Palau has over 200 lush, uninhabited limestone islands scattered across crystal-clear waters.
- Palau is home to some of the largest giant clams in the world, their vibrant colors lighting up the ocean floor like underwater rainbows.
- Dive sites are littered with sunken ships and planes from World War II, offering a hauntingly beautiful glimpse into history.
- Milky Way Lagoon: This natural spa is filled with limestone mud, said to have healing properties.
- The mysterious stone monoliths of Badrulchau on Babeldaob Island puzzle historians. They're like Palau's version of Stonehenge.
- Palau protects its manta rays with a special sanctuary. Snorkeling here, you might see these gentle giants gliding through the water.
- On Babeldaob Island, there's a vine swing known as the Tarzan Swing, where you can really swing into a river like a movie hero.
- Ngardmau Waterfall is the largest waterfall in Palau, located in a lush jungle.
- Etpison Museum showcases Palau's culture, history, and natural wonders, including traditional art and World War II relics.

Mandarin fish

Where in the world is Palau ...

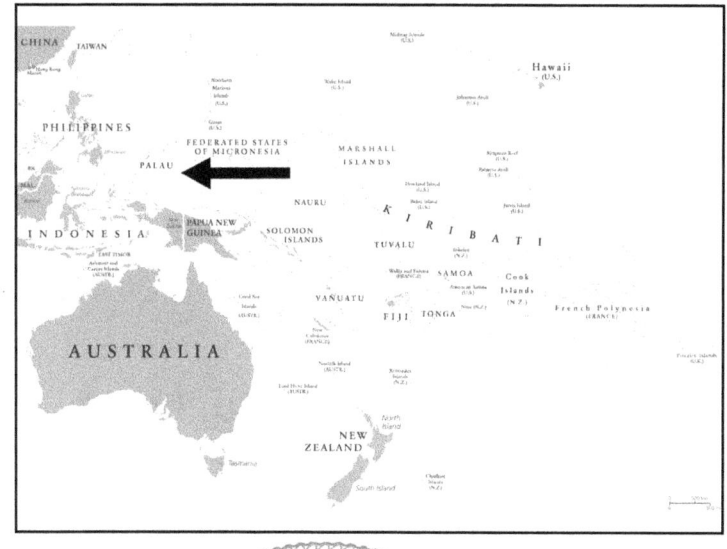

Rock Islands

Word Scramble
Unscramble the letters to reveal the words.

1. RIPACLTO   _ _ _ _ _ _ _

2. FICAPCI CEONA   _ _ _ _ _ _ _ _ _ _ _

3. LIEHFJLSY KAEL   _ _ _ _ _ _ _ _ _ _ _ _ _

4. RVTANNCIOOSE   _ _ _ _ _ _ _ _ _ _

5. LUGUNEMDR   _ _ _ _ _ _ _ _

6. OTSEN SLMOOHITN _ _ _ _ _ _ _ _ _ _ _ _ _

7. OKCR SINSLDA   _ _ _ _ _ _ _ _ _ _ _

8. RMDANAGU TWFRLELAA _ _ _ _ _ _ _ _ _ _ _ _ _ _ _ _

9. LNOSETMEI   _ _ _ _ _ _ _ _ _

10. NGTIA MALSC   _ _ _ _ _ _ _ _ _ _

11. LKIMY AYW ALGOON _ _ _ _ _ _ _ _ _ _ _ _ _ _

12. NENKUS SPISH   _ _ _ _ _ _ _ _ _ _ _

PAPUA NEW GUINEA

Papua New Guinea is a country of extraordinary diversity, home to rugged mountains, dense rainforests, and more than 800 languages, making it one of the world's most linguistically diverse places. Its landscapes are inhabited by numerous tribes who maintain ancient customs and traditions. Celebrated through vibrant festivals like the Sing-sing, these traditions showcase music, dance, and elaborate costumes, reflecting the rich cultural heritage of the country. Papua New Guinea's remote wilderness is also a haven for unique wildlife.

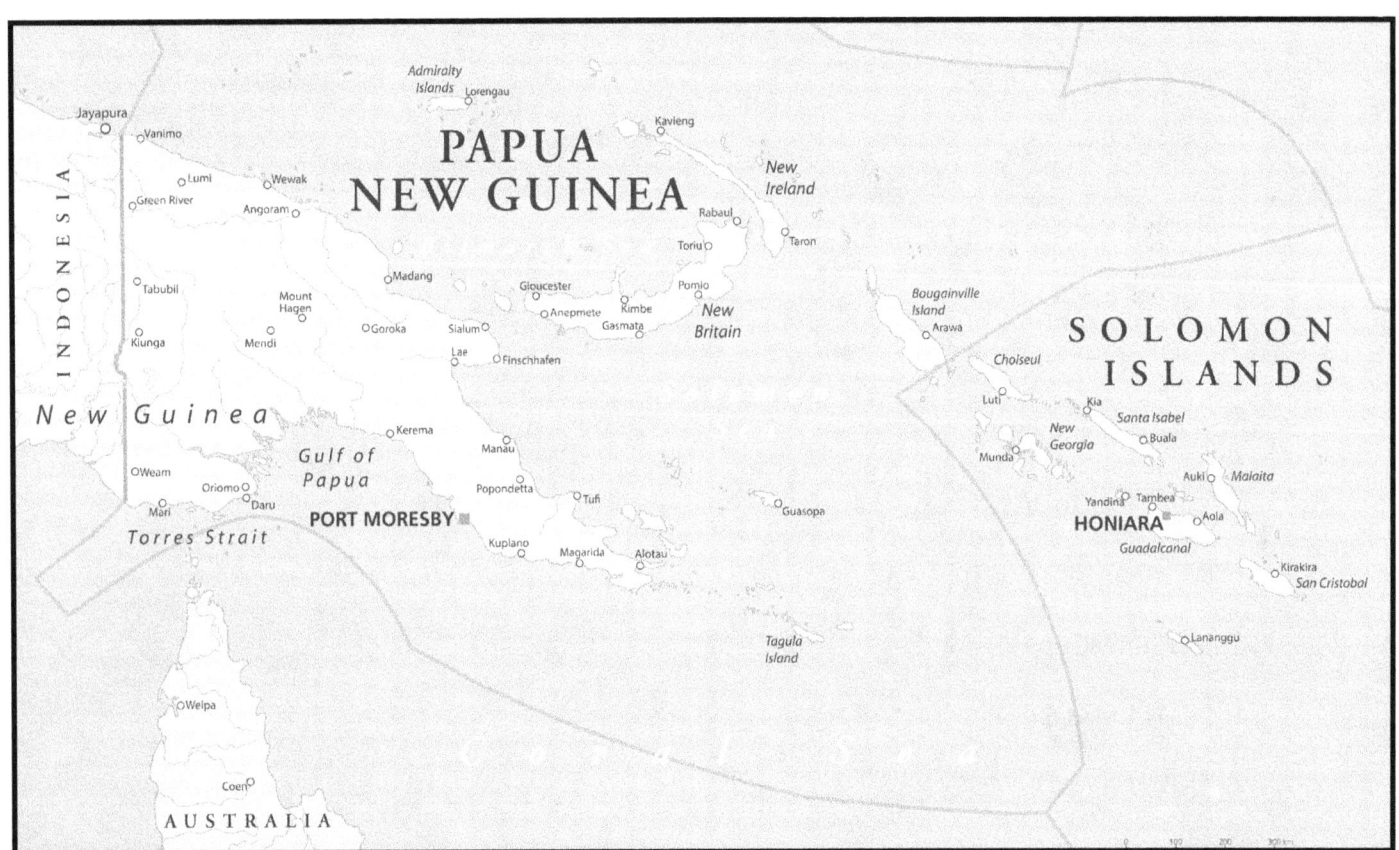

Facts About Papua New Guinea

Capital: Port Moresby
National Motto: Unity in Diversity
Area: 178,704 square miles (462,840 square kilometers)
Major Cities: Port Moresby, Lae, Arawa
Population: 10.34 million
Bordering Countries: Maritime borders with Australia, Micronesia, Solomon Islands, New Caledonia
Languages: Tok Pisin, English, Hiri Motu
Major Landmarks: Kokoda Track, Mount Wilhelm, Sepik River, Port Moresby Nature Park
Famous Papua New Guineans: Michael Somare (prime minister), Dame Carol Kidu (politician), Dika Toua (weightlifter)

Country Flag

Did You Know?

- Papua New Guinea is home to the stunning Birds of Paradise, known for their vibrant colors and unique dances.
- Over 800 languages are spoken here, making it the most linguistically diverse country in the world.
- The Kokoda Track is a challenging 96-kilometer trail that crosses the Owen Stanley Range. Trekking it is like stepping back in time, following the footsteps of soldiers from WWII.
- Mud Men of Asaro: Famous for their eerie mud masks and body paint, the Mud Men create an unforgettable sight.
- Mount Wilhelm, the highest peak in Papua New Guinea, offering breathtaking views from the top.
- Sing-Sing Festivals are vibrant cultural festivals where tribes gather to sing, dance, and show off their unique traditions.
- Sepik River is one of the longest rivers in the world. It flows through swamps, tropical rainforests, and mountains.
- A "tumbuna" is a gathering where people wear traditional dress and celebrate ancient customs.
- The Crocodile Festival celebrates the crocodile, an important cultural symbol.

National Emblem

Where in the world is Papua New Guinea ...

Traditional Sing-Sing Festival

Dugong

Across

1 Famous trekking route in Papua New Guinea (6)

5 Popular traditional dance (4-4)

9 Name of the large river found in Papua New Guinea (5)

10 Colorful bird found in Papua New Guinea (4,2,8)

Down

2 National animal of Papua New Guinea (6)

3 Capital of Papua New Guinea (4,7)

4 Highest mountain in Papua New Guinea (5,7)

6 An important cultural symbol (9)

7 Papua New Guinea is known for its _____ (9)

8 Official language of Papua New Guinea (7)

Crossword Puzzle

PITCAIRN ISLANDS

The Pitcairn Islands are a group of four volcanic islands in the southern Pacific Ocean, known as the last British Overseas Territory in the Pacific. These remote islands are best known for being the refuge of the mutineers from the HMS Bounty in 1789. Today, Pitcairn is home to a small community that descends from the mutineers and their Tahitian companions. The islands offer a unique and untouched natural environment, with rugged landscapes and a rich marine ecosystem.

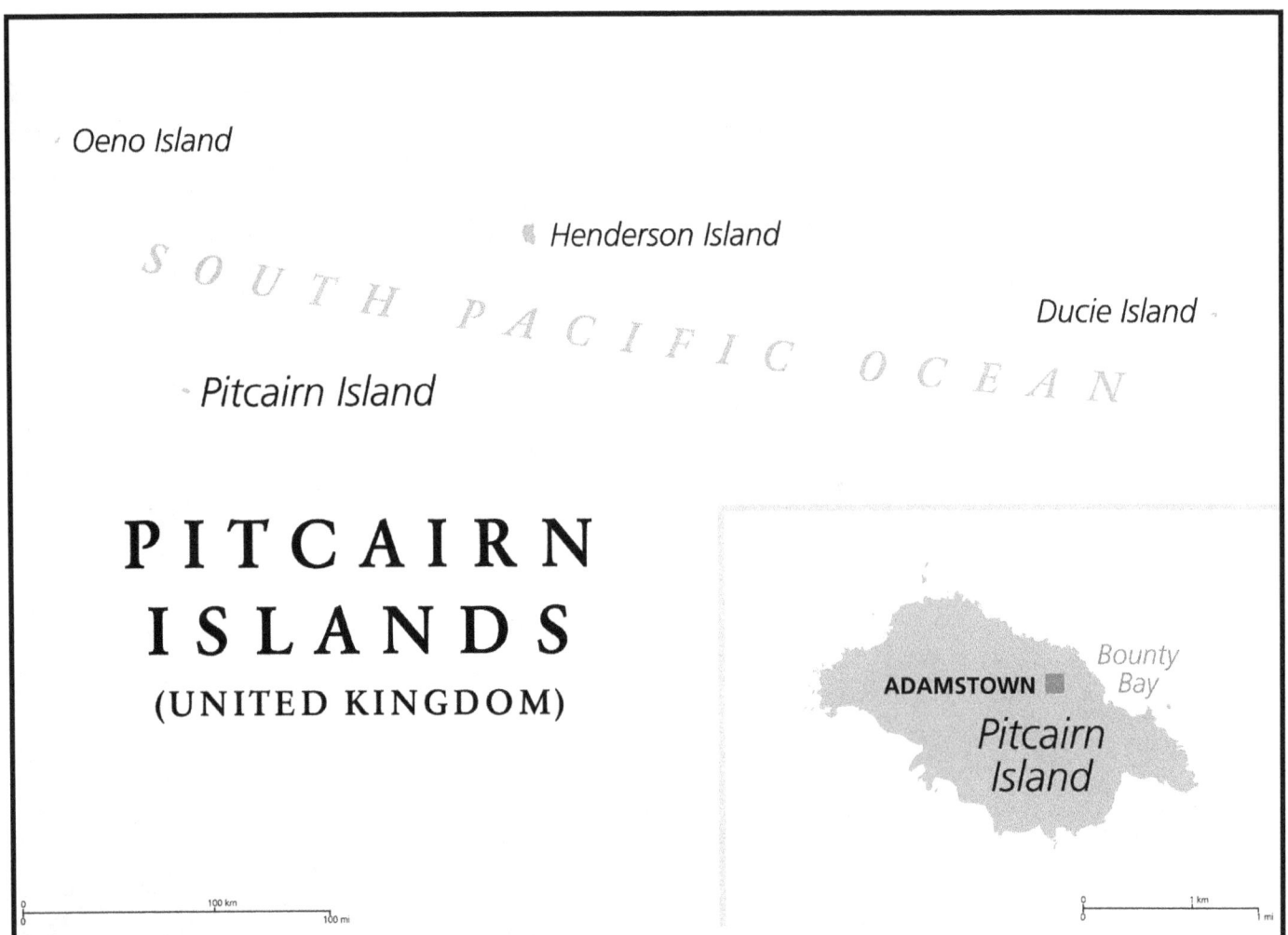

Facts About Pitcairn

Capital:	Adamstown
National Motto:	No official motto
Area:	19 square miles (49 square kilometers)
Islands:	Pitcairn, Henderson, Ducie, and Oeno Islands
Population:	50
Bordering Countries:	None
Languages:	Pitkern, English
Major Landmarks:	Bounty Bay, St. Paul's Pool, Christian's Cave
Famous Pitcairns:	Fletcher Christian (mutineer), John Adams (mutineer), Meralda Warren (artisan), Tom Christian (radio operator)

Country Flag

Did You Know?

- The Pitcairn Islands are home to fewer than 50 people, making it one of the least populated territories in the world.
- The residents are descendants of the Bounty mutineers and their Tahitian companions.
- Pitcairn is famous for its collectible postage stamps, a major source of income.
- Every year on January 23, the islanders celebrate the arrival of their ancestors with a reenactment and feast.
- There's no airport on Pitcairn, so the only way to visit is by a long boat ride.
- Henderson Island: This UNESCO World Heritage Site is an untouched paradise for rare birds and plants but is also highlighted for the sad accumulation of plastic pollution, showing the global impact on even the most remote places.

HMS Bounty

Where in the world are Pitcairn Islands ...

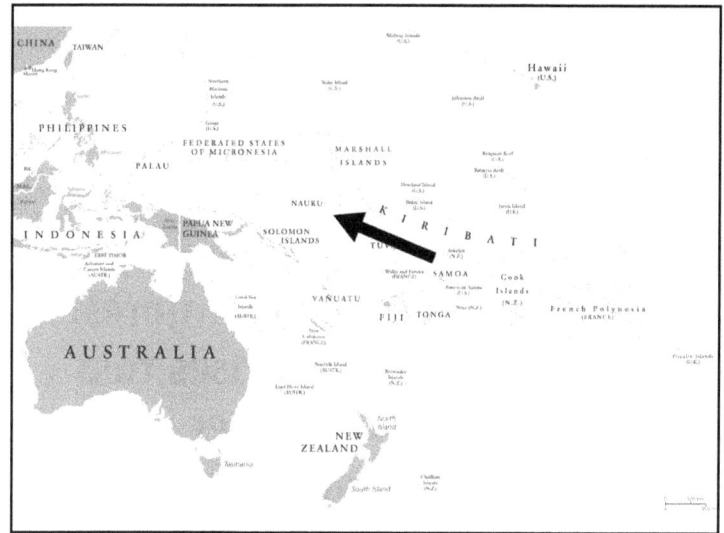

Postage Stamp

Pandanus Tree

Word Scramble
Unscramble the letters to reveal the words.

1. NVCAILOC ALIDNSS   _ _ _ _ _ _ _ _ _ _ _ _ _ _
2. TDNEUI IOKDGMN   _ _ _ _ _ _ _ _ _ _ _ _
3. NEEIRMSUT   _ _ _ _ _ _ _ _ _
4. SHM NBUTOY   _ _ _ _ _ _ _ _ _
5. AWNSMDOAT   _ _ _ _ _ _ _ _
6. TNBOUY AYB   _ _ _ _ _ _ _ _ _
7. SEEDHONRN SALDIN   _ _ _ _ _ _ _ _ _ _ _ _ _ _ _
8. TELRFCHE CHAISTRIN _ _ _ _ _ _ _ _ _ _ _ _ _ _ _ _ _
9. APANUNSD ETER   _ _ _ _ _ _ _ _ _ _ _ _
10. PGAESOT PMTSSA   _ _ _ _ _ _ _ _ _ _ _ _ _
11. REMOET   _ _ _ _ _ _
12. NMEAIR ETSOMYSESC _ _ _ _ _ _ _ _ _ _ _ _ _ _ _ _

SAMOA

Samoa is an island country in the South Pacific Ocean, known for its natural beauty, from sparkling waterfalls and lush rainforests to stunning beaches and volcanic landscapes. It comprises two main islands, Upolu and Savai'i, along with several smaller islands. Samoa's rich culture is celebrated through traditional ceremonies, music, dance, and the famous tattooing art known as 'tatau.' The Samoan way of life, or "Fa'a Samoa," emphasizes community, respect for the environment, and a deep connection to ancestral traditions, playing a central role in the daily lives of its people.

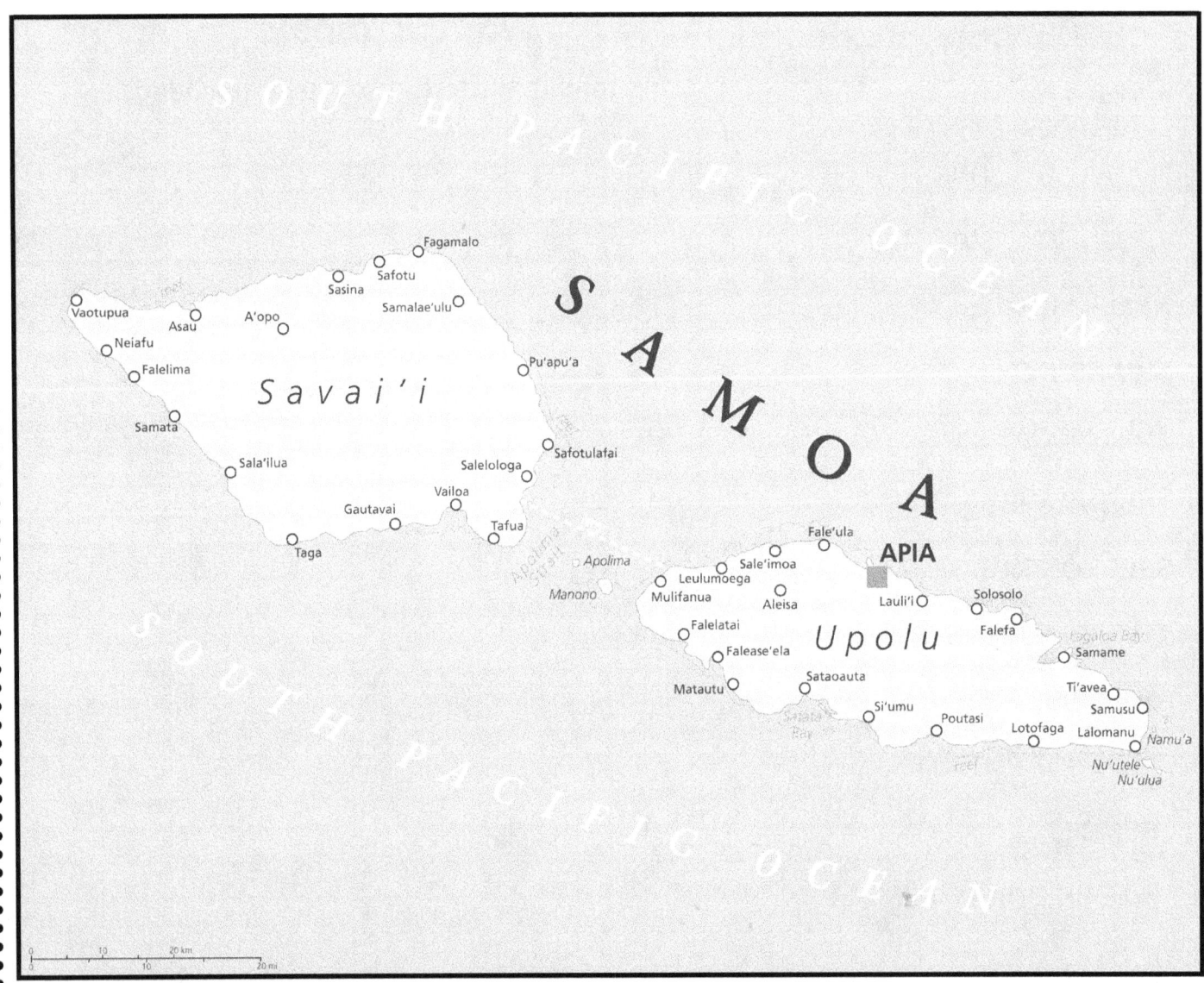

Facts About Samoa

Capital:	Apia
National Motto:	God be the Foundation of Samoa
Area:	1,097 square miles (2,842 square kilometers)
Major Cities:	Apia, Asau, Mulifanua
Population:	218,764
Bordering Countries:	No direct borders
Languages:	Samoan, English
Major Landmarks:	To Sua Ocean Trench, Papase'ea Sliding Rocks, Lalomanu Beach, Piula Cave Pool, Robert Louis Stevenson Museum
Famous Samoans:	Nuufolau Joel Seanoa (wrestler), David Tua (boxer), Albert Wendt (writer)

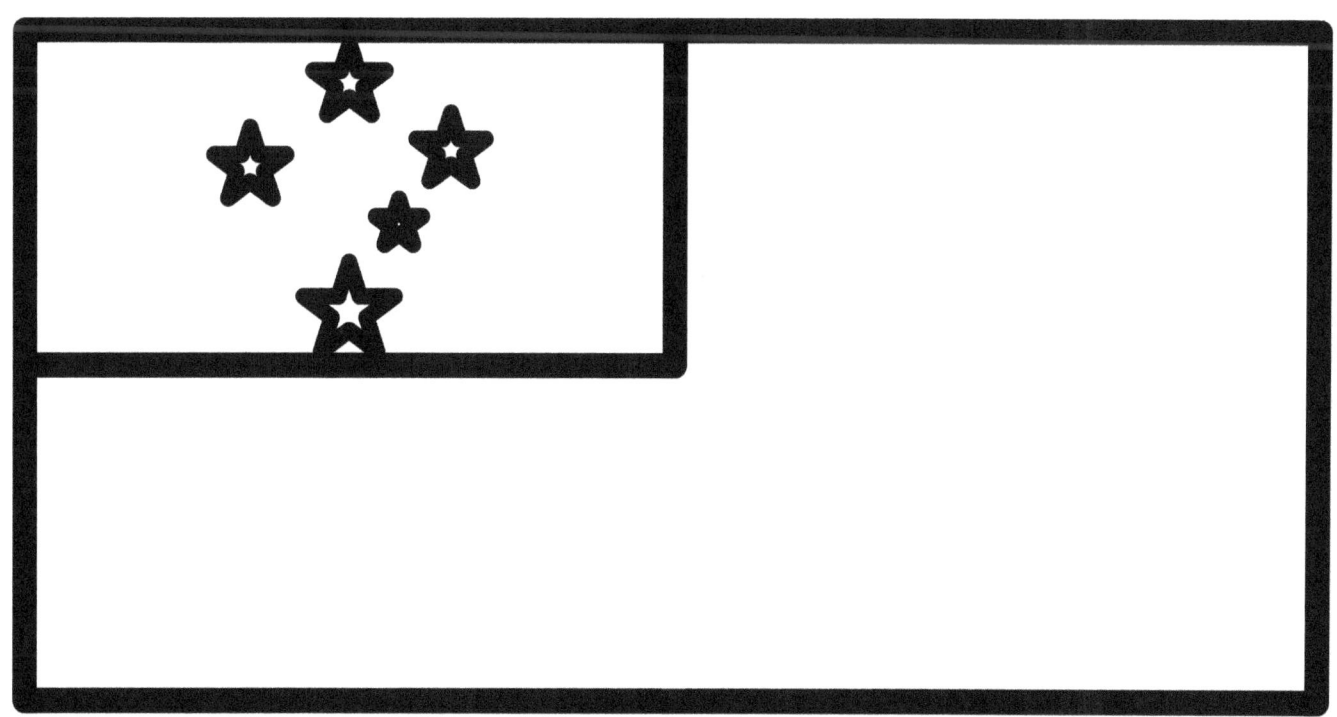

Country Flag

Did You Know?

- Samoa is considered the birthplace of traditional Polynesian tattoos, known as "tatau," a practice with deep cultural significance that dates back over 2,000 years.
- Alofaaga Blowholes in Savai'i shoot sea water up to hundreds of feet in the air when waves crash into them, creating natural geysers.
- Sunday in Samoa is a day of rest and worship, with most of the country attending church services and spending time with family in observance of cultural and religious practices.
- Samoa switched its position on the International Date Line in 2011 to be the first to welcome the day, aligning its business days more closely with New Zealand and Australia.
- The Siva Afi, or fire knife dance, is a traditional Samoan dance that involves twirling a knife with both ends on fire, showcasing skill and bravery.
- To Sua Ocean Trench is a massive natural swimming hole with crystal-clear waters, accessible by a ladder. Swimming here is like floating in a hidden world.
- Samoa's lush rainforests are home to unique species of flora and fauna, including flying foxes, which are actually large fruit bats.

National bird: Manumea

Where in the world is Samoa ...

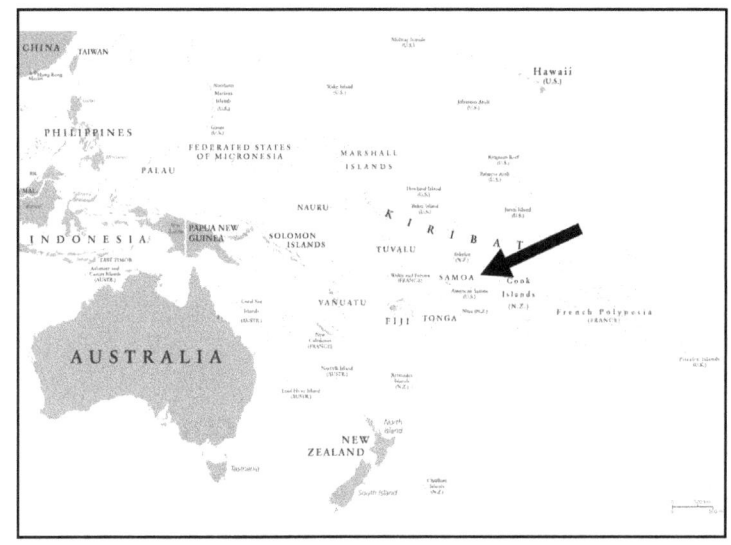

Traditional Samoan Fale

Word Search

APIA
CULTURE
FLYING FOX
MANUMEA
RAINFOREST
SAMOA
SAVAII
SIVA AFI
TATTOOS
UPOLU
VOLCANOES
WATERFALLS

```
V R C U T S S E O N A C L O V
Y N W G M Z K Y O Z L J T L K
D S M E H A D D T E C P A R J
U L O P U H N G G T S I T O A
E B L L C K P U S T I Q T N R
R Y A X Z B N E M A M K O M Z
U S A U U H R I V E J K O X V
T R S N A O Q A L N A T S O S
L O X I F O S Q F F N Y V F N
U U A N V T B W B C L O A G A
C E I A A A V S A M O A Q N P
U A U G P S A S A E B V D I F
R U V Y I L W F F R R Q C Y Y
Y G F Z A X C N I R Q V T L M
I W A T E R F A L L S L O F D
```

SOLOMON ISLANDS

The Solomon Islands, located in the South Pacific, are a collection of nearly 1,000 islands and atolls known for their lush tropical forests, beautiful beaches, and rich biodiversity. This nation is steeped in history, with significant World War II sites, and is renowned for its vibrant Melanesian culture, which includes traditional music, dance, and crafts. The islands offer spectacular diving opportunities, with coral reefs, wartime wrecks, and abundant marine life. The Solomon Islands' diverse ecosystems and cultures make it a unique destination where ancient customs coexist with modern life.

Facts About Solomon Islands

Capital: Honiara
National Motto: To Lead Is to Serve
Area: 11,157 square miles (28,896 square kilometers)
Major Cities: Honiara, Gizo, Auki, Kirakira
Population: 707,851
Bordering Countries: Maritime borders with Papua New Guinea, Vanuatu, Australia, Nauru, Tuvalu
Languages: English, Solomons' Pijin
Major Landmarks: Kennedy Island, Honiara Solomon Peace Memorial Park, Marovo Lagoon, Mount Popomanaseu
Famous Solomon Islanders: Peter Kenilorea (prime minister), Ellison Pogo (bishop), Jeniifer Wate (singer)

Country Flag

Did You Know?

- The Solomon Islands are home to giant rats and megabats, real-life creatures that seem straight out of a storybook.
- Iron Bottom Sound, the stretch of ocean between Guadalcanal and the Florida Islands, is a graveyard of WWII ships and planes, now a popular dive site.
- Active and dormant volcanoes dot the landscape, with Kavachi, an underwater volcano, known for its eruptions and shark inhabitants.
- Known for their incredibly friendly and welcoming people, the Solomon Islands are often called the "Happy Isles."
- Dense, untouched rainforests cover much of the islands, harboring rare plants and animals unique to the region.
- Kennedy Island: Named after John F. Kennedy, this small island marks the spot where the future US president was marooned during WWII after PT-109 was sunk.
- Marovo Lagoon is the largest saltwater lagoon in the world, surrounded by a double barrier reef.
- Home to ancient shrines with human skulls, Skull Island offers a glimpse into the headhunting past of the local culture.

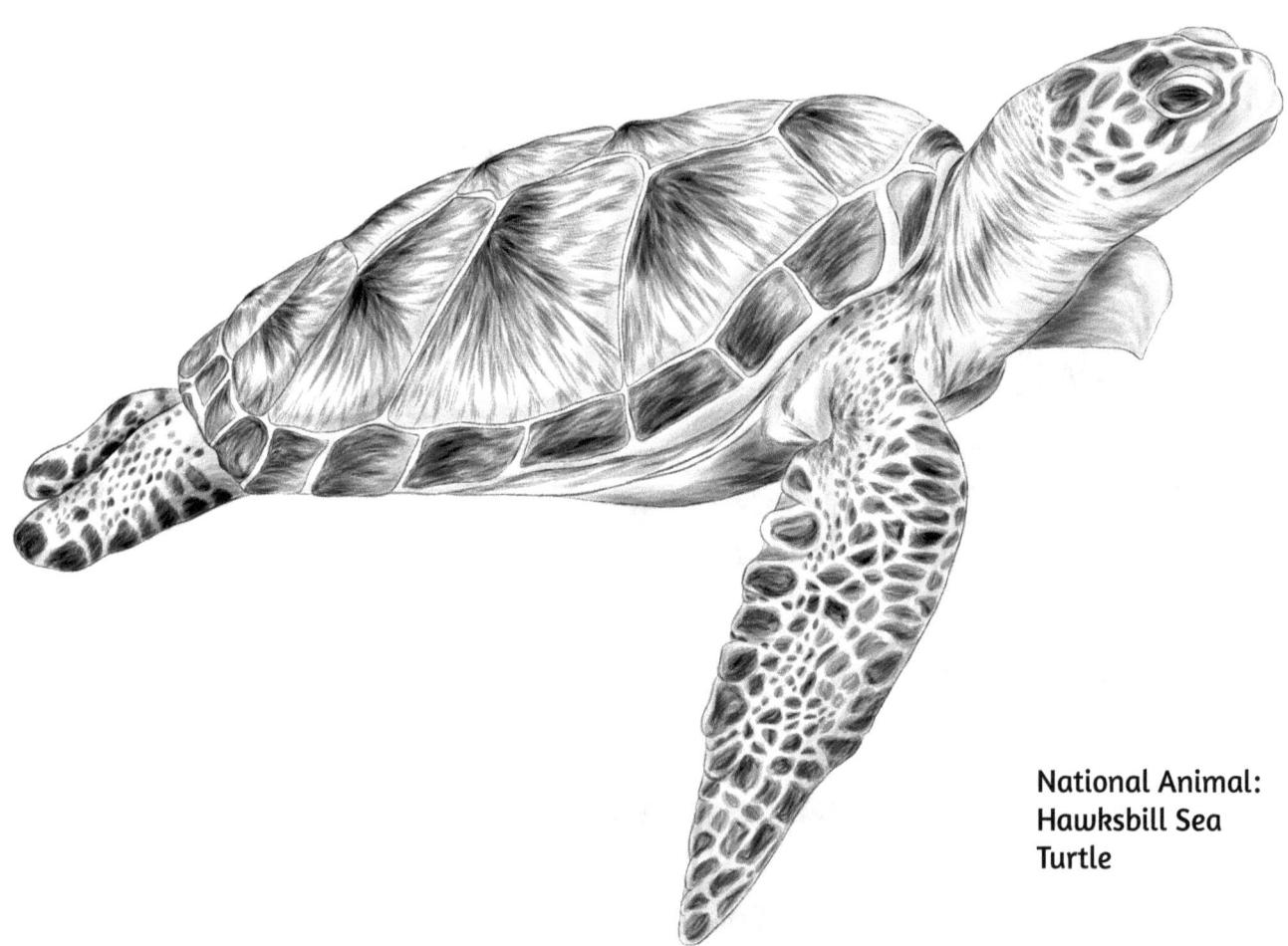

National Animal: Hawksbill Sea Turtle

Where in the world are Solomon Islands ...

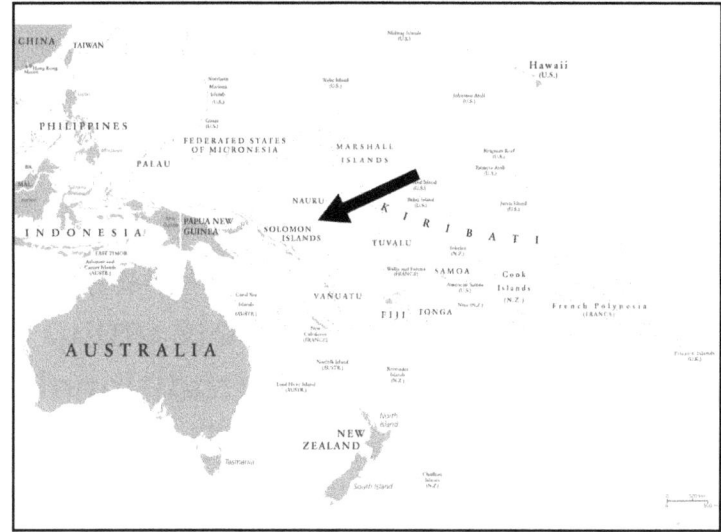

National Plant: Sea Hibiscus

Word Scramble

Unscramble the letters to reveal the words.

1. LOOMSON ADSNLSI _ _ _ _ _ _ _   _ _ _ _ _ _ _
2. OUHTS FIAPICC _ _ _ _ _   _ _ _ _ _ _ _
3. CLOTAPRI RSTOSEF _ _ _ _ _ _ _ _   _ _ _ _ _ _ _
4. IDSBIRIYOTVE _ _ _ _ _ _ _ _ _ _ _
5. SAENENILMA LREUUTC _ _ _ _ _ _ _ _ _   _ _ _ _ _ _ _ _
6. NRAIHOA _ _ _ _ _ _
7. YKNEDNE LNSDIA _ _ _ _ _ _ _   _ _ _ _ _ _
8. MOAROV NOOLAG _ _ _ _ _ _   _ _ _ _ _ _
9. EAS UHBISICS _ _ _   _ _ _ _ _ _ _
10. NIOR TOBOMT OUDSN _ _ _ _   _ _ _ _ _ _   _ _ _ _ _
11. AHAKVCI AVNOLOC _ _ _ _ _ _ _   _ _ _ _ _ _ _
12. PYPHA SESLI _ _ _ _ _   _ _ _ _ _

TOKELAU

Tokelau is a territory of New Zealand located in the South Pacific Ocean, consisting of three tropical coral atolls. This remote group of islands is known for its strong community spirit and traditional Polynesian culture, which is reflected in the daily lives of its inhabitants. Tokelau is self-sufficient and relies heavily on fishing and subsistence farming, with coconut being a significant crop. Despite its isolation, Tokelau is making strides in renewable energy, aiming to become powered almost entirely by solar energy. Life in Tokelau is closely connected to the ocean and the environment, with a deep respect for nature ingrained in its culture.

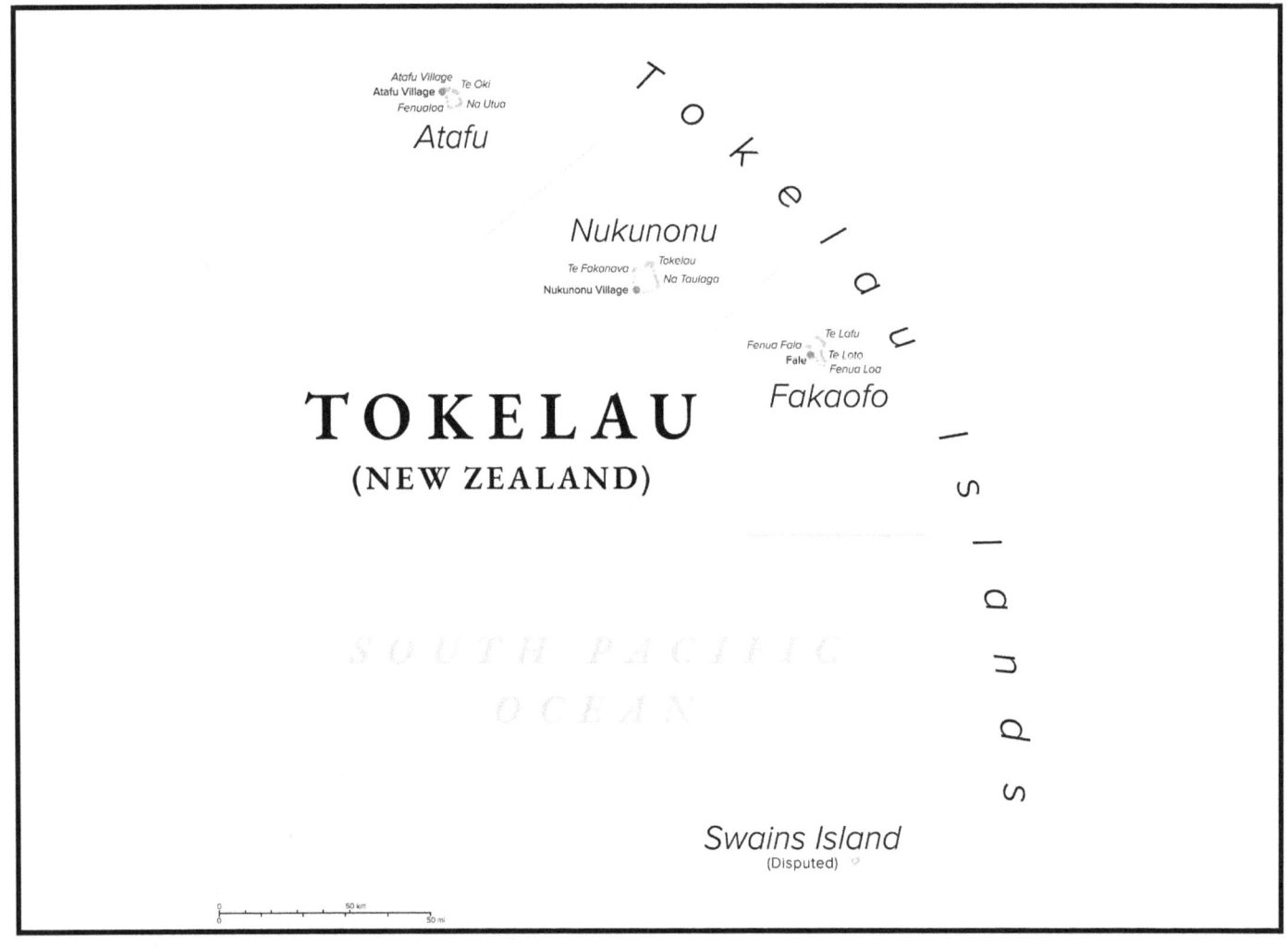

Facts About Tokelau

Capital:	None
National Motto:	No official motto
Area:	4.6 square miles (12 square kilometers)
Major Towns:	Atafu, Nukunonu, Fakaofo
Population:	1,909
Bordering Countries:	Samoa, Tuvalu
Languages:	Tokelauan and English
Major Landmarks:	Atafu Atoll, Nukunonu Atoll, Fakaofo Atoll, Tokelau National Library and Archives
Famous Tokelauans:	Opetaia Foa'i (singer), Pita Alatini (rugby player), Courtney Meredith (writer)

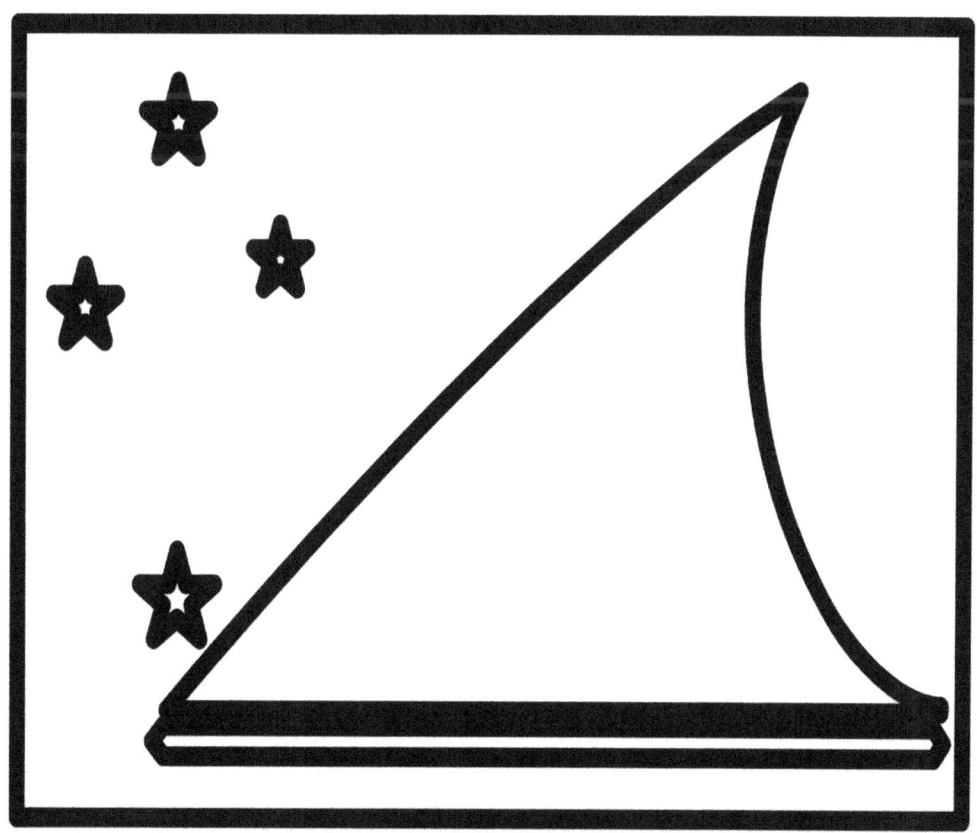

Country Flag

Did You Know?

- Tokelau is made up of three atolls: Atafu, Nukunonu, and Fakaofo, each with its own unique community and way of life.
- Tokelau is the first 100% solar-powered territory in the world, using renewable energy to light up all its homes and buildings.
- There are no airports in Tokelau. To get there, you need to take a boat ride from Samoa, which can take about a day.
- The waters around Tokelau are teeming with fish, making fishing a crucial part of daily life and sustenance for the islanders.
- Each atoll in Tokelau governs itself through a system of local councils, with decisions made collectively for the benefit of all.
- Coconuts are vital to Tokelau, used for food, drink, and making copra (dried coconut meat) for export. Life on the islands is closely tied to these versatile trees.
- Being low-lying atolls, Tokelau is at risk from rising sea levels due to climate change, making its sustainability efforts even more critical.
- Traditional Polynesian canoes are a common sight, reflecting the importance of the sea for transportation, fishing, and cultural identity in Tokelau.

Where in the world is Tokelau ...

Traditional vaka canoe

Crossword Puzzle

Across

2 Type of vehicle needed to get to Tokelau (4)

5 Tokelau is located in this region of the Pacific Ocean (9)

7 Number of atolls that make up Tokelau (5)

9 Type of government in Tokelau (5,8)

10 Name of one of the three atolls (5)

Down

1 Main crop in Tokelau (7)

3 Tokelau is territory of this country (3,7)

4 Popular activity and source of food (7)

6 Type of energy used in Tokelau (5)

8 Type of traditional canoe (4)

TONGA

Tonga, officially known as the Kingdom of Tonga, is a Polynesian sovereign state and archipelago comprising 171 islands, of which 36 are inhabited. Located in the South Pacific Ocean, it's the only remaining Polynesian monarchy. Tonga is known for its unique blend of traditional culture and modernity, with ancient Polynesian customs still playing a significant role in social and political life. The islands offer stunning natural landscapes, including volcanic formations, tropical rainforests, and pristine beaches. Tongans are renowned for their hospitality, vibrant cultural events like the Heilala Festival, and sports, especially rugby, which is a national passion.

Facts About Tonga

Capital:	Nuku'Alofa
National Motto:	God and Tonga Are My Inheritance
Area:	289 square miles (750 square kilometers)
Major Cities:	Nuku'Alofa, Neiafu
Population:	106,017
Bordering Countries:	Maritime borders with Fiji, Samoa, Cook Islands
Languages:	Tongan, English
Major Landmarks:	Ha'amonga 'a Maui, Mapu'a 'a Vaea Blowholes, Eua National Park, Tongatapu Lagoon
Famous Tongans:	Pita Taufatofua (Olympian), 'Akilisi Pohiva (politician), George Tupou V (king), Taniela Tupou (rugby)

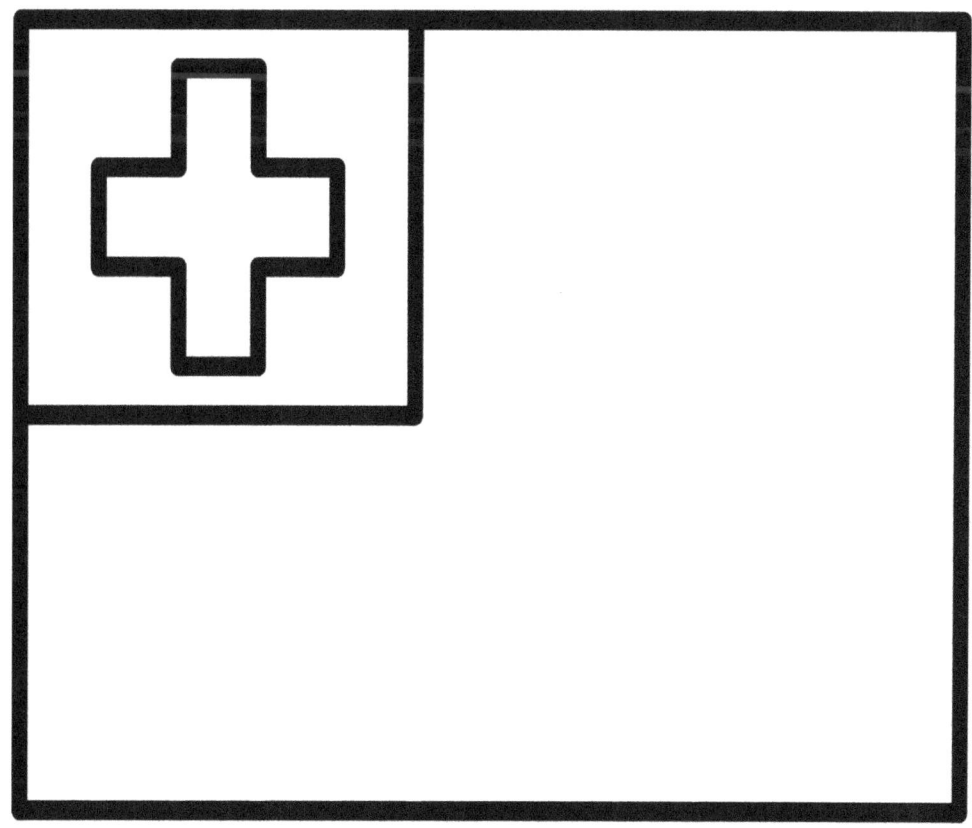

Country Flag

Did You Know?

- Tonga is the only remaining monarchy in the Pacific, with a royal family that traces its history back over 1,000 years.
- In 2015, an underwater volcano eruption in Tonga created a new island, offering scientists a rare chance to study how life begins to inhabit new land.
- Tonga is home to the flying fox, a type of fruit bat considered sacred and protected by royal decree. Seeing them soar through the skies is a common and majestic sight.
- Ha'amonga 'a Maui is a Stonehenge-like structure made from massive limestone slabs, believed to have been built in the 13th century as an entrance to the royal compound or as a calendar.
- Rugby is a national passion in Tonga, with the national team, the 'Ika-le Tahi (Sea Eagles), known for their fierce competitiveness and skill on the international stage.

Coat of arms

Where in the world is Tonga ...

Flying fox

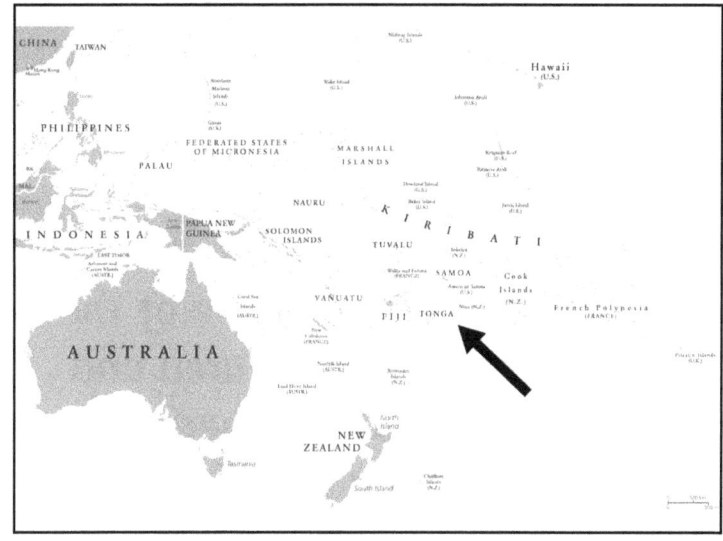

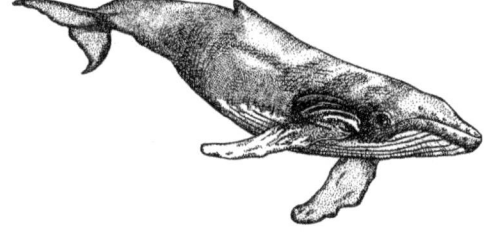

Humpback whale

Word Scramble

Unscramble the letters to reveal the words.

1. RAIALPHGCOE   _ _ _ _ _ _ _ _ _ _
2. HMRACNOY   _ _ _ _ _ _ _
3. PLIATHOITYS   _ _ _ _ _ _ _ _ _ _
4. AAIHLLE ISETAFVL   _ _ _ _ _ _ _ _ _ _ _ _ _ _
5. AVE OLINNAAT RKPA   _ _ _ _ _ _ _ _ _ _ _ _ _
6. NOPTGATAU LANOGO   _ _ _ _ _ _ _ _ _ _ _ _ _ _
7. NGIYFL OXF   _ _ _ _ _ _ _ _ _
8. UCAHBMPK AELHW   _ _ _ _ _ _ _ _ _ _ _ _ _
9. EAS SEELAG   _ _ _ _ _ _ _ _
10. GKNMOID FO NATOG   _ _ _ _ _ _ _ _ _ _ _ _ _
11. SPDALECANS   _ _ _ _ _ _ _ _ _
12. NUFAEI   _ _ _ _ _ _

TUVALU

Tuvalu is a small island nation in the Pacific Ocean, consisting of nine islands. It's known for its low-lying atolls and is one of the smallest countries in the world, both in terms of land area and population. Despite its size, Tuvalu has a rich cultural heritage, with traditional music, dance, and crafts playing a significant role in community life. The nation faces challenges from rising sea levels due to climate change, making environmental preservation a key focus. Tuvaluans live closely with nature, relying on fishing and agriculture, and are known for their strong community spirit and hospitality.

TUVALU

Nanumea
Niutao
Nanumanga
Nui
Asau
Nukufetau
SOUTH
Funafuti
PACIFIC
Nukulaelae
OCEAN
Niulakita

Facts About Tuvalu

Capital:	Funafuti
National Motto:	Tuvalu for the Almighty
Area:	10.04 square miles (26 square kilometers)
Major Cities:	Funafuti
Population:	11,204
Bordering Countries:	Maritime borders with Kiribati, Tokelau, Samoa, Fiji, Solomon Islands, Nauru
Languages:	Tuvaluan and English
Major Landmarks:	Funafuti Atoll, Funafuti Conservation Area, Te Namo Lagoon
Famous Tuvaluans:	Enele Sopoaga (politician), Sir Tomasi Puapua (Governor-General), Sir Kamuta Latasi (prime minister), Taukiei Kitara (environmentalist)

Country Flag

Did You Know?

- Tuvalu is famous for being on the front lines of climate change, with rising sea levels posing a significant threat to its very existence.
- "Tuvalu" means "eight standing together," referring to the country's eight traditionally inhabited islands.
- Tuvalu is one of the few countries in the world without any rivers or streams. Freshwater is precious here!
- The Tuvalu flag features nine stars, representing each of the country's islands, including one for the tiny uninhabited island of Niulakita.
- Falekaupule Festival is an important cultural festival involves traditional dancing, singing, and feasting, showcasing Tuvalu's rich heritage and community spirit.
- Tuvalu is known for issuing colorful and collectible postage stamps, a significant source of revenue and a collector's delight worldwide.
- When the highest tides, known as King Tides, occur, Tuvaluans celebrate with festivals, even as these tides highlight the threat of sea-level rise.
- The "fatele" is a traditional Tuvaluan dance accompanied by songs and performed at community events, showcasing the vibrancy of Tuvaluan culture.

Coat of arms

Where in the world is Tuvalu ...

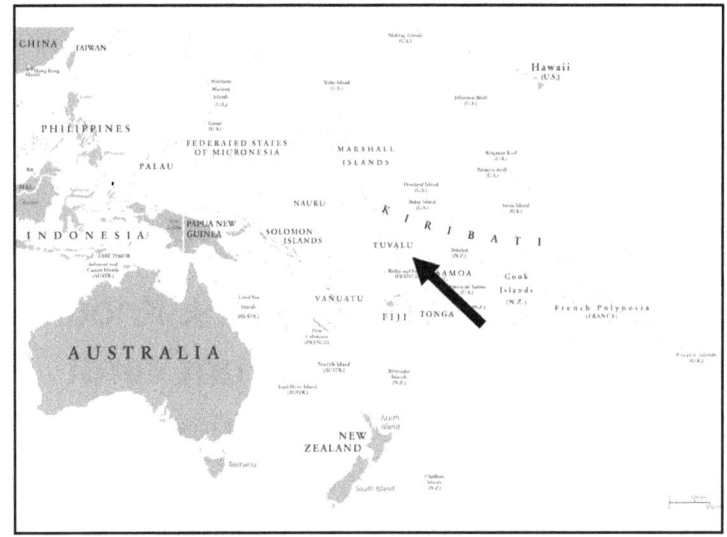

National flower:
Plumeria

National animal:
Spotted dolphin

Word Search

AGRICULTURE
CLIMATE CHANGE
DOLPHINS
FATELE
FESTIVALS
FISHING
FUNAFUTI
HOSPITALITY
KING TIDES
NIULAKITA
STAMPS
TUVALU

```
L G L G P T I W D C Y C J N G
C L I M A T E C H A N G E G U
H U Y I A T M D O L P H I N S
G Y Q S G G J J V Z W H T J S
N B V Q F Z R M Q Y B U N L T
A Y T I L A T I P S O H A S N
T W F W W K T K C T C V F E K
I O I M R I D E S U I F F N K
K W S L E N N T L T L K X U Q
A S H H L G T S S E L T L R P
L P I L H T Y E E G C A U Y E
U M N M W I F F T U V E P R V
I A G P L D V D V U Q C M X E
N T E V T E D H T D H G W N O
R S A T X S I T U F A N U F V
```

VANUATU

Vanuatu is an island nation located in the South Pacific Ocean, made up of around 80 islands that stretch 1,300 kilometers. Known for its volcanic landscapes, beautiful beaches, and vibrant coral reefs, Vanuatu offers a mix of thrilling adventures and peaceful nature experiences. The culture is rich and diverse, with the Ni-Vanuatu people maintaining many of their traditional customs and practices. Vanuatu is famous for its ceremonial land diving, a precursor to bungee jumping, and for being home to several active volcanoes, including Mount Yasur, which is accessible to tourists. The country's commitment to sustainable tourism and preservation of its unique culture and natural resources makes it a fascinating destination.

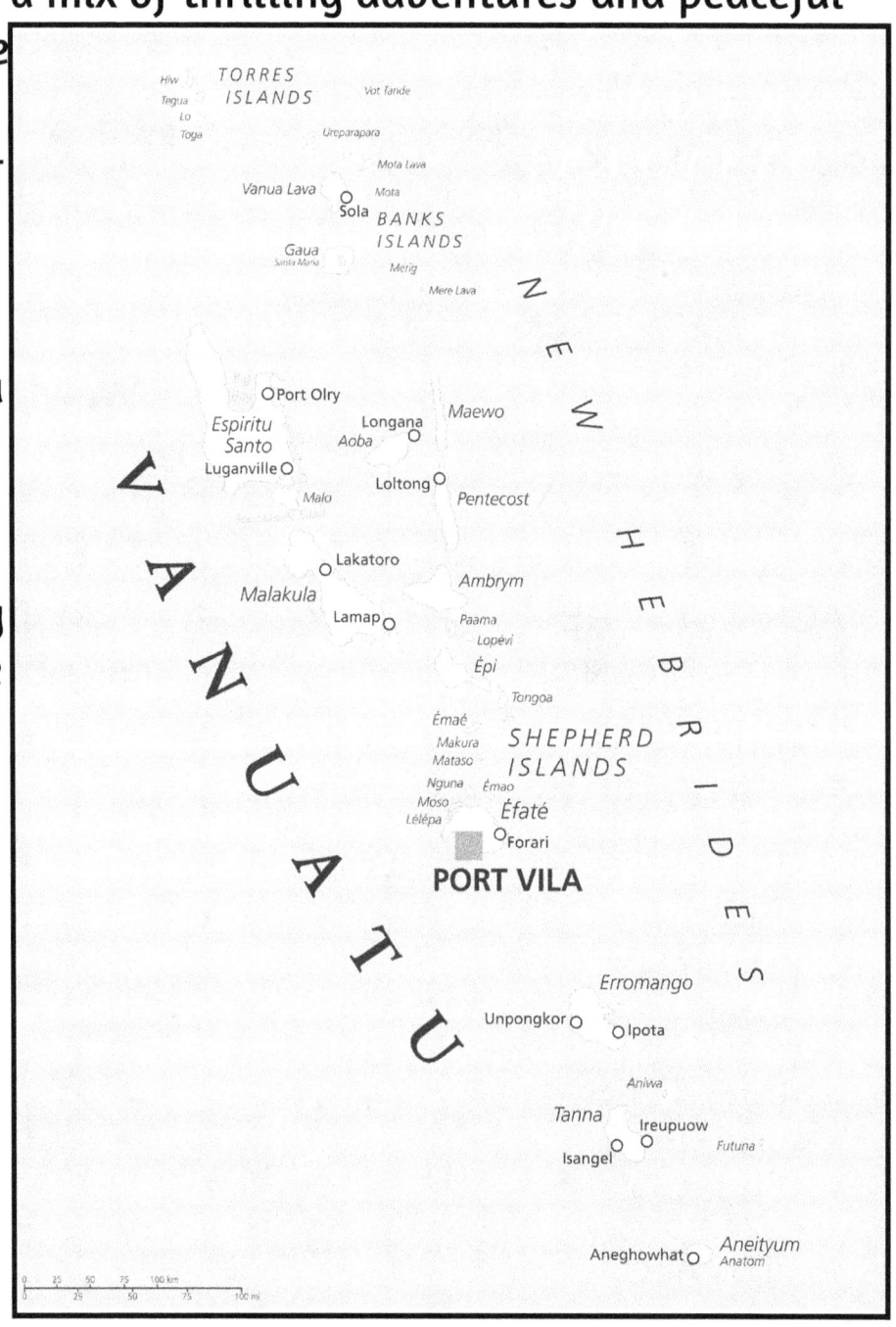

Facts About Vanuatu

Capital:	Port Vila
National Motto:	In God We Stand
Area:	4,707 square miles (12, 190 square kilometers)
Major Cities:	Port Vila, Luganville, Saratamata
Population:	319,137
Bordering Countries:	Maritime borders with Fiji, New Caledonia, Solomon Islands and Australia
Languages:	Bislama, English, French
Major Landmarks:	Mount Yasur, Millennium Cave, Mele Cascades
Famous Vanuatuans:	Father Walter Lini (prime minister), Sethy Regenvanu (cultural influencer), Ralph Regenvanu (politician), Vanessa Quai (singer)

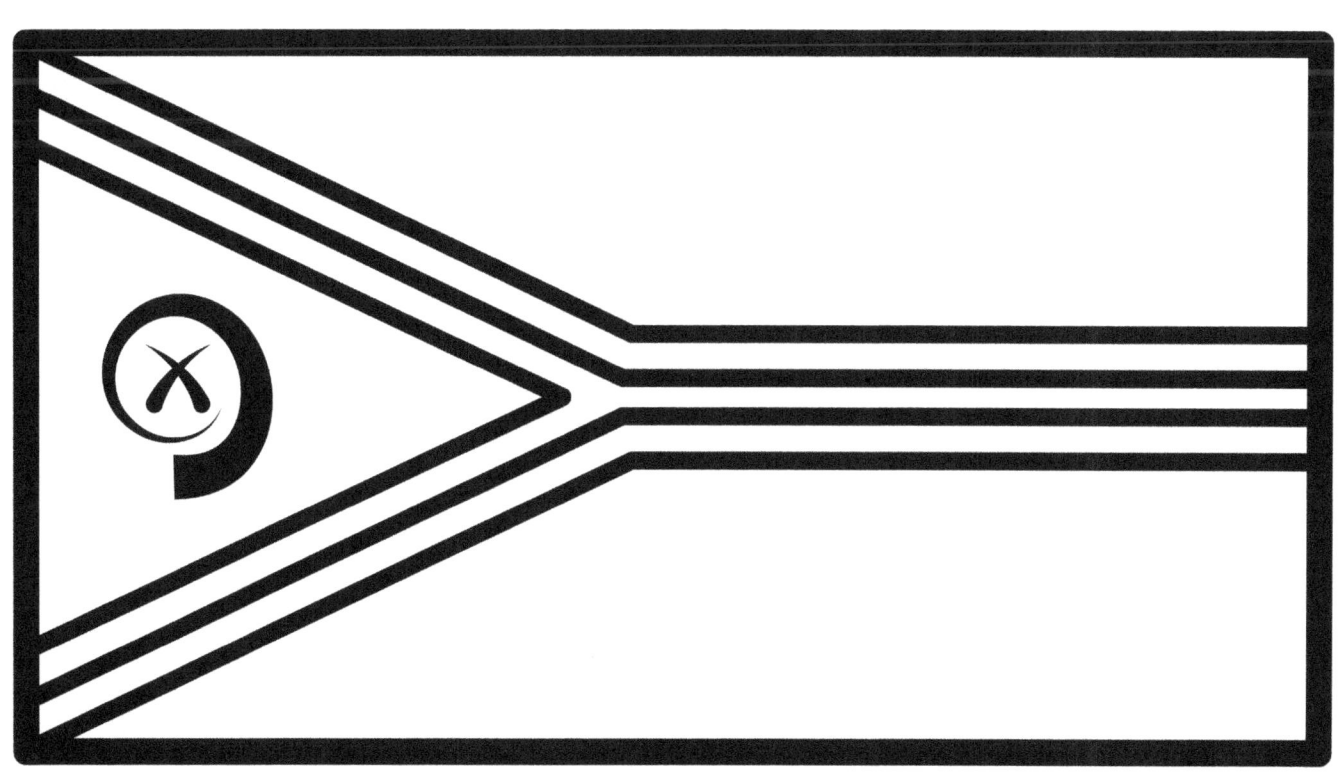

Country Flag

Did You Know?

- Vanuatu is home to several active volcanoes, including Mount Yasur, one of the most accessible active volcanoes in the world. Visitors can stand on the rim and watch the spectacular lava show.
- In the crystal-clear waters of Vanuatu lies an underwater post office, off the coast of Hideaway Island. You can actually send waterproof postcards from here!
- Vanuatu boasts one of the largest banyan trees in the world. This massive tree covers an area that could fit over 50 cars beneath its canopy.
- The waters around Vanuatu are a diver's paradise, with vibrant coral reefs teeming with marine life, including the famous SS President Coolidge wreck dive site.
- Vanuatu's Sand Drawings: Recognized by UNESCO, these intricate sand drawings are not only art but also a complex form of communication and storytelling among the islands' communities.
- Natural freshwater springs known as blue holes can be found in Vanuatu, with crystal-clear, deep blue water that's pure enough to drink and beautiful for swimming.
- The people of Tanna Island practice an ancient tradition of fire walking, which is considered a sacred ritual and a test of strength and endurance.

Mount Yasur

LONG GOD YUMI STANAP

Where in the world is Vanuatu...

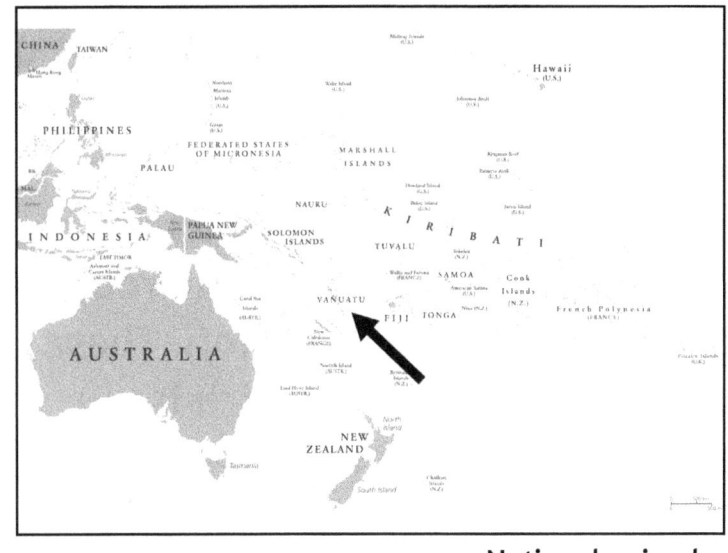

Banyan tree

National animal: Iguana

Word Scramble

Unscramble the letters to reveal the words.

1. LAORC FESER _ _ _ _ _   _ _ _ _ _
2. DALN IVNDGI _ _ _ _   _ _ _ _ _
3. UMOTN ASYRU _ _ _ _ _   _ _ _ _ _
4. RPTO AIVL _ _ _ _   _ _ _ _
5. DSEERPHH NASIDSL _ _ _ _ _ _ _ _   _ _ _ _ _ _
6. NNMIEIMLUL EACV _ _ _ _ _ _ _ _ _   _ _ _ _
7. EMLE SASCCEAD _ _ _ _   _ _ _ _ _ _ _
8. TUAVUNNASA _ _ _ _ _ _ _ _
9. YNANBA ERET _ _ _ _ _ _   _ _ _ _
10. IFRE KLWINGA _ _ _ _   _ _ _ _ _ _ _
11. DIAYEAHW DISLNA _ _ _ _ _ _ _ _   _ _ _ _ _ _
12. ANDS GNRSDAIW _ _ _ _   _ _ _ _ _ _ _

WALLIS AND FUTUNA

Wallis and Futuna is a French overseas collectivity composed of three main volcanic tropical islands and a number of tiny islets, located in the South Pacific Ocean. It's split into two island groups: Wallis, the larger group, and Futuna with the smaller Alofi. These islands are known for their rich Polynesian culture, which is vividly expressed through traditional dances, music, and ceremonies. Despite being a part of France, Wallis and Futuna retain a unique cultural identity, with a strong community life centered around the Catholic Church and ancient Polynesian royalty. The landscape features lush forests, pristine beaches, and clear lagoons, offering a tranquil and relatively untouched natural environment.

WALLIS AND FUTUNA
(FRANCE)

Facts About Wallis and Futuna

Capital: Matā'utu
National Motto: Liberty, Equality, Fraternity
Area: 106 square miles (274 square kilometers)
Major Towns: Matā'utu, Liku, Alele, Falaleu
Population: 11,151
Bordering Countries: Maritime borders with Tuvalu, Fiji, Tonga, Samoa, Tokelau
Language: French
Major Landmarks: Talietumu, Lake Lalolalo, Mata-Utu Cathedral, Alofi Island, Mont Puke
Famous Wallisians and Futunians: Patalione Kanimoa (mayor), Sylvain Brial (politician), Mikaele Tuugahala (rugby player), Aloisiae Fai'ivae (deacon)

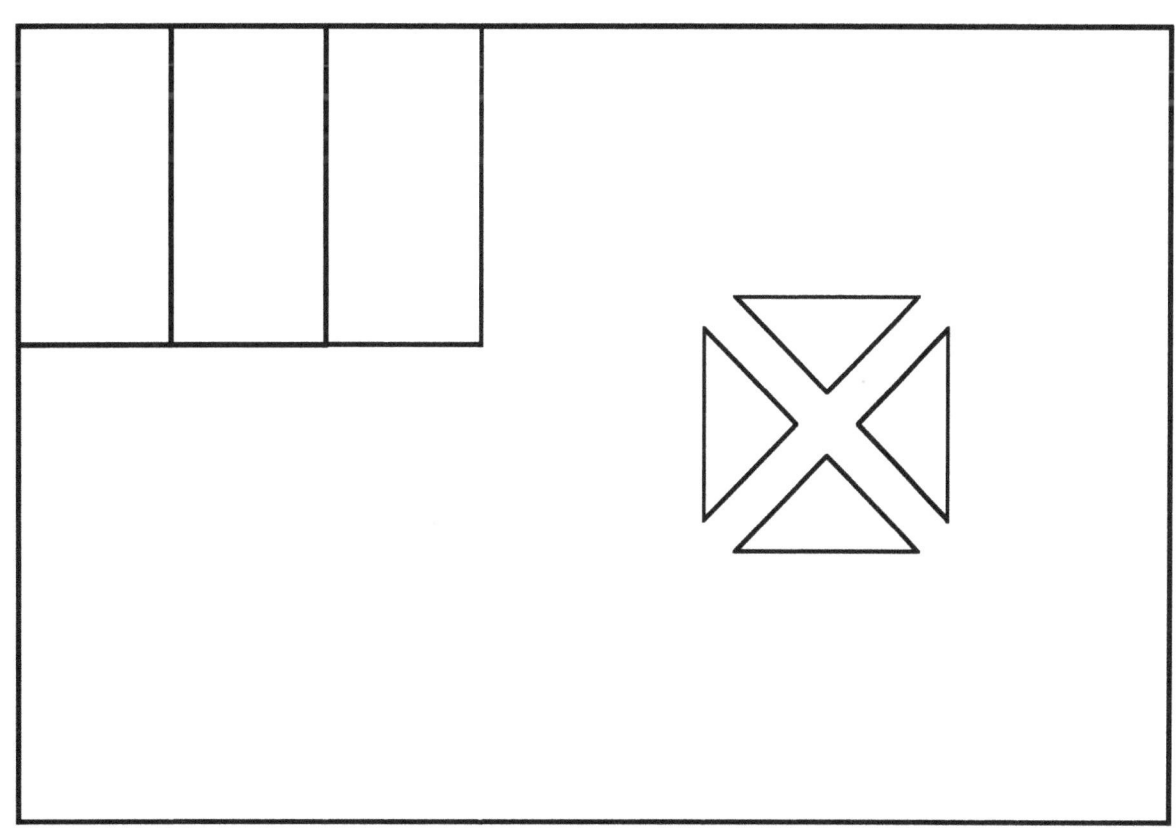

Country Flag

Did You Know?

- The territory is divided into three traditional kingdoms, each ruled by its own king and supported by a system of chiefs and clans.
- The waters around Wallis and Futuna are rich in marine biodiversity, protected by law to preserve their pristine condition for future generations.
- Often described as the most dramatic of Wallis's crater lakes, Lake Lalolalo is almost perfectly circular with steep sides, resembling a giant natural well.
- Futuna is the final resting place of St. Pierre Chanel, the first martyr of Oceania and a patron saint of the Pacific, whose shrine attracts pilgrims from across the region.
- The art of canoe building is alive and well in Futuna, where traditional Polynesian outrigger canoes are still made using age-old techniques, showcasing the islanders' deep connection to the sea.
- The islands are home to unique species of plants and animals, including several types of birds and marine life that are not found anywhere else in the world.

Word Scramble

Unscramble the letters to reveal the words.

1. LOHCACTI UHCHRC _ _ _ _ _ _ _ _ _ _ _ _ _ _
2. HOONR ASLDSIN _ _ _ _ _ _ _ _ _ _ _ _
3. TUOHS APFCCII _ _ _ _ _ _ _ _ _ _ _ _
4. TELATUIUM _ _ _ _ _ _ _ _ _
5. ELAK LAOLALLO _ _ _ _ _ _ _ _ _ _ _ _
6. LAFOI AIDSLN _ _ _ _ _ _ _ _ _ _ _
7. MIRNAE EIODIVSRYBTI _ _ _ _ _ _ _ _ _ _ _ _ _ _ _ _ _ _
8. RPRIEE LACEHN _ _ _ _ _ _ _ _ _ _ _ _
9. OCENA IBDNLGIU _ _ _ _ _ _ _ _ _ _ _ _ _
10. IWLSLA NDA NFUUAT _ _ _ _ _ _ _ _ _ _ _ _ _ _ _
11. ESOYAPNIL _ _ _ _ _ _ _ _ _
12. TILSOSRECVYILEETVCAO _

Where in the world is Wallis and Futuna ...

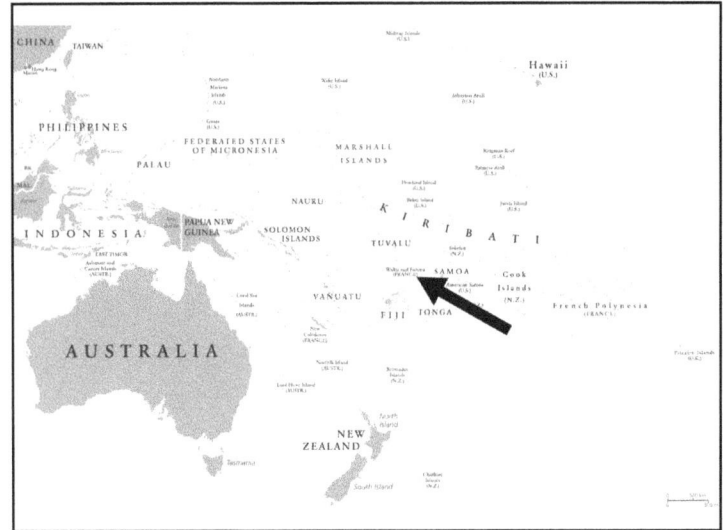

St. Pierre Chanel

Crossword Puzzle

Across

3 Wallis and Futuna are part of this country (6)
4 Climate of Wallis and Futuna (8)
6 Religion in Wallis and Futuna (8)
7 Language spoken in Wallis and Futuna (6)
8 The larger of the two islands groups (6)

Down

1 Capital of Wallis and Futuna (4,3)
2 Patron saint (6,6)
5 Third main island in Wallis and Futuna (5)
6 Popular type of boat in Wallis and Futuna (5)

Use the numbered map to fill in the names of the countries and territories below.

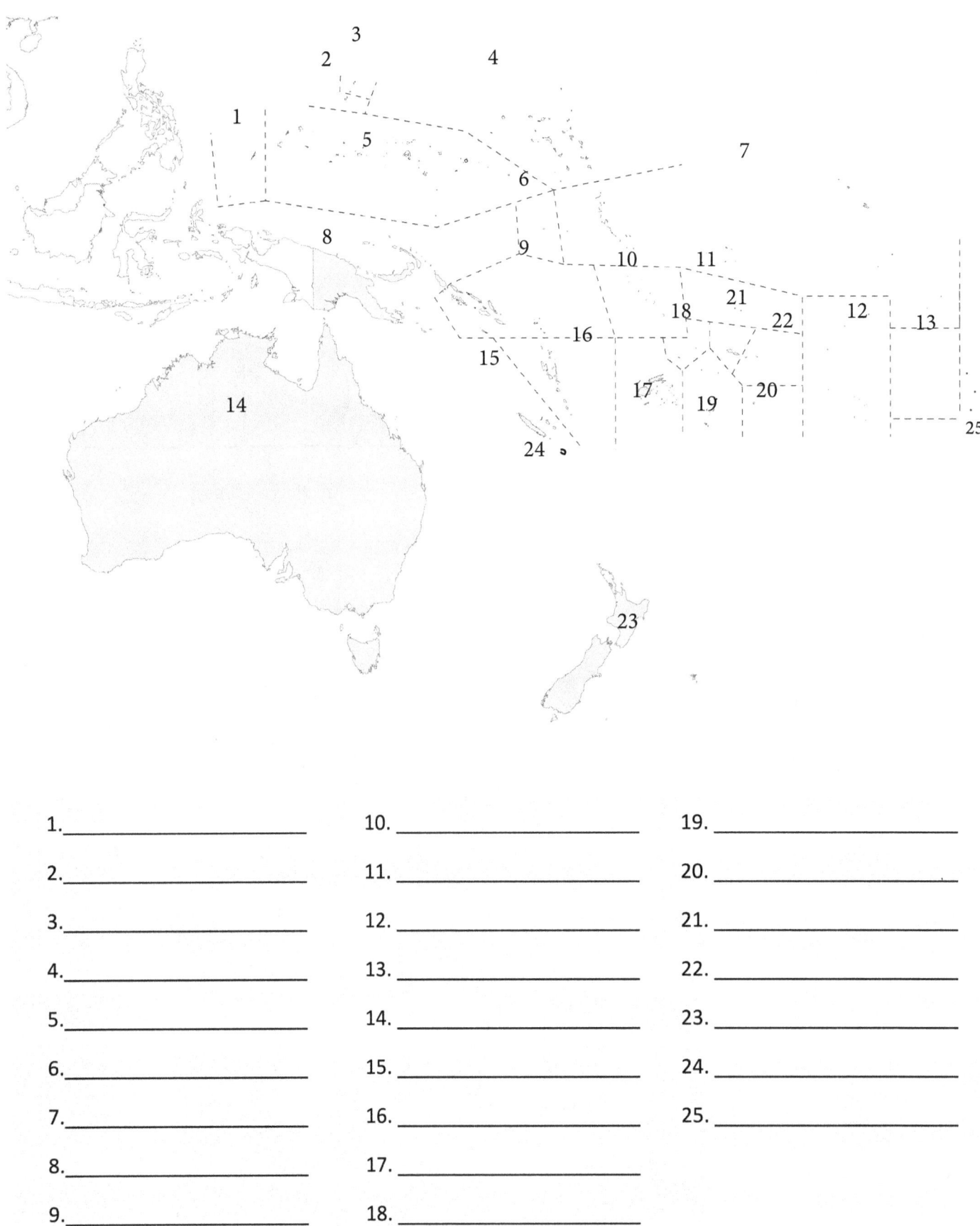

1. _____
2. _____
3. _____
4. _____
5. _____
6. _____
7. _____
8. _____
9. _____
10. _____
11. _____
12. _____
13. _____
14. _____
15. _____
16. _____
17. _____
18. _____
19. _____
20. _____
21. _____
22. _____
23. _____
24. _____
25. _____

Country Capitals

Write the capital for each country or territory.

1. American Samoa (US territory) _____
2. Australia _____
3. Cook Islands (Associated state of New Zealand) _____
4. Federated States of Micronesia _____
5. Fiji _____
6. French Polynesia (French overseas collectivity) _____
7. Guam (US territory) _____
8. Kiribati _____
9. Marshall Islands _____
10. Nauru _____
11. New Caledonia (French territory) _____
12. New Zealand _____
13. Niue (Associated state of New Zealand) _____
14. Norfolk Island (Australian external territory) _____
15. Northern Mariana Islands (US territory) _____
16. Palau _____
17. Papua New Guinea _____
18. Pitcairn Islands (British Overseas Territory) _____
19. Samoa _____
20. Solomon Islands _____
21. Tokelau (Territory of New Zealand) _____
22. Tonga _____
23. Tuvalu _____
24. Vanuatu _____
25. Wallis and Futuna (French overseas collectivity) _____

- Adamstown
- Alofi
- Apia
- Avarua
- Canberra
- Funafuti
- Hagåtña
- Honiara
- Kingston
- Majuro
- Mata-Utu
- Ngerulmud
- Nouméa
- Nuku'alofa
- Pago Pago
- Palikir
- Papeete
- Port Moresby
- Port Vila
- Saipan
- Suva
- Tarawa
- Wellington
- Yaren

Answers

1. Australia
2. Federated States of Micronesia, Marshall Islands, Kiribati, Solomon Islands, Papua New Guinea
3. New Zealand
4. Papua New Guinea
5. Indian Ocean
6. Pitcairn Islands
7. Tasmanian Sea
8. Possible answers: Australia, Papua New Guinea, New Zealand, Fiji, the Solomon Islands, Federated States of Micronesia, Vanuatu, Samoa, Kiribati, Tonga, the Marshall Islands, Palau, Tuvalu, and Nauru

1. Kangaroo
2. Koala
3. Platypus
4. Dingo
5. Emu
6. Wombat
7. Tasmanian devil
8. Echidna
9. Saltwater crocodile
10. Kookaburra

Giant clam, Humphead wrasse, Kingfisher, Sea turtle, Reef shark, Coconut crab

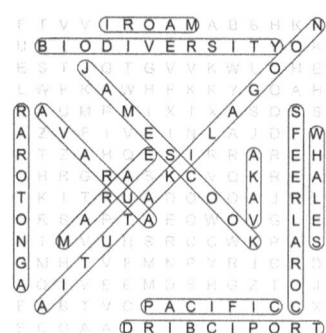

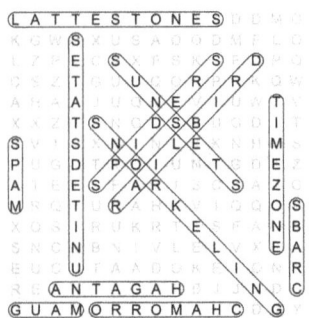

Kiwi, Hector's dolphin, Tuatara, Kakapo, Little blue penguin, Sheep

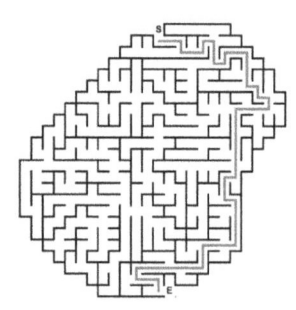

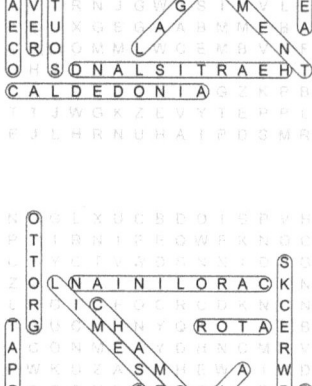

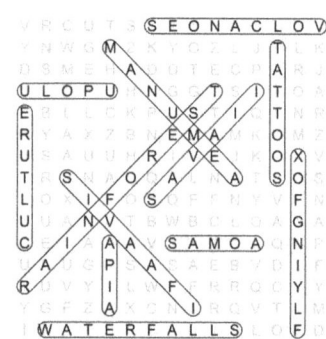

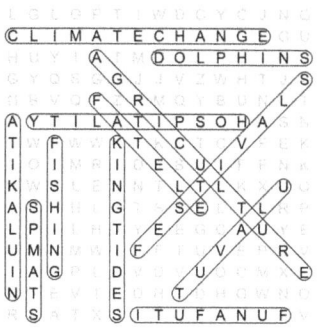

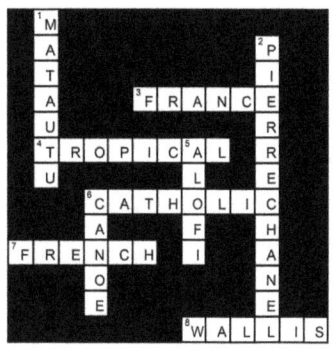

1. Palau 2. Guam 3. Northern Mariana Islands 4. Marshall Islands 5. Federated States of Micronesia 6. Nauru 7. Kiribati 8. Papua New Guinea 9. Solomon Islands 10. Tuvalu 11. Tokelau 12. Cook Islands 13. French Polynesia 14. Australia 15. New Caledonia 16. Vanuatu 17. Fiji 18. Wallis and Futuna 19. Tonga 20. Niue 21. Samoa 22. American Samoa 23. New Zealand 24. Norfolk Islands 25. Pitcairn Islands

Capitals

American Samoa – Pago Pago
Australia - Canberra
Cook Islands - Avarua
Federated States of Micronesia - Palikir
Fiji - Suva
French Polynesia - Papeete
Guam - Hagåtña
Kiribati - Tarawa
Marshall Islands - Majuro
Nauru - Yaren
New Caledonia - Nouméa
New Zealand - Wellington
Niue - Alofi
Norfolk Island - Kingston
Northern Mariana Islands - Saipan
Palau - Ngerulmud
Papua New Guinea - Port Moresby
Pitcairn Islands - Adamstown
Samoa - Apia
Solomon Islands - Honiara
Tokelau - None
Tonga - Nuku'alofa
Tuvalu - Funafuti
Vanuatu - Port Vila
Wallis and Futuna - Mata-Utu

www.ingramcontent.com/pod-product-compliance
Lightning Source LLC
Chambersburg PA
CBHW081200020426
42333CB00020B/2583